THE WHITE
HORSE KING

The Life of Alfred the Great

BEN MERKLE

THOMAS NELSON
Since 1798

NASHVILLE   DALLAS   MEXICO CITY   RIO DE JANEIRO   BEIJING

Published in Nashville, Tennessee, by Thomas Nelson. Thomas Nelson is a registered trademark of Thomas Nelson, Inc.

Thomas Nelson, Inc. titles may be purchased in bulk for educational, business, fund-raising, or sales promotional use. For information, please e-mail SpecialMarkets@ThomasNelson.com.

Maps on pages 7 and 171 are inspired by maps in Richard Abels' *Alfred the Great*.
Map on page 43 is inspired by a map in Ryan Lavelle's *Fortifications in Wessex c. 800–1066*.
Map on page 147 is inspired by a map in Alfred P. Smyth's *King Alfred the Great*.

Library of Congress Control Number: 2009935985

ISBN: 978-1-5955-5252-5

Printed in the United States of America

09 10 11 12 RRD 6 5 4 3 2 1

FOR BEKAH

Hwa þeos, þe gesihþ swa swa se morgen
Fæger swa se mona
Beorht swa se sunne
Torhtmod swa se scildweall.

Before the gods that made the gods
Had seen their sunrise pass,
The White Horse of the White Horse Vale
Was cut out of the grass.

Before the gods that made the gods
Had drunk at dawn their fill,
The White Horse of the White Horse Vale
Was hoary on the hill.

Age beyond age on British land,
Æons on æons gone,
Was peace and war in western hills,
And the White Horse looked on.

For the White Horse knew England
When there was none to know;
He saw the first oar break or bend,
He saw heaven fall and the world end,
O God, how long ago.

—FROM G. K. CHESTERTON's *The Ballad of the White Horse*

Contents

Family Tree

Æthelwulf (king of Wessex AD 839–858)
married first to Osburh and then to Judith

CHILDREN OF ÆTHELWULF AND OSBURH:
Æthelstan
Æthelbald (king of Wessex AD 858–860)
Æthelswith (married to Burgred, king of Mercia)
Æthelberht (king of Wessex AD 860–865)
Æthelred (king of Wessex AD 865–871)
Alfred (king of the Anglo-Saxons AD 871–899), married to Ealswith
(died AD 902)

ALFRED'S CHILDREN:
Æthelflæd (queen of Mercia, died AD 918) married to Æthelred
(ealdorman of Mercia AD 880–911)
Edward the Elder (king of the Anglo-Saxons AD 899–924)
Æthelgifu (abbess of Shaftesbury)
Ælfthryth married to Baldwin (count of Flanders)
Æthelweard

Edward's son was Æthelstan (king of the Anglo-Saxons AD 924–939)

Chronology

AD 410: Visigoths attack Rome, causing Emperor Honorius to abandon Roman Britain.

AD 410–600: Migration of the Angles, Saxons, and Jutes from the continent to the island of Britain.

AD 597: Augustine of Canterbury takes office and begins the Christianization of the Anglo-Saxons.

AD 635: Aidan founds a monastery on Lindisfarne.

AD 684: Cuthbert becomes bishop of Lindisfarne.

AD 793: Vikings raid Lindisfarne.

AD 839: Æthelwulf becomes king of Wessex.

AD 849: Alfred is born in Wantage.

AD 853: Alfred is sent to Rome, and his mother, Osburh, dies.

AD 855: Alfred travels to Rome once more with his father.

AD 858: Æthelwulf dies, and the crown passes to Æthelbald.

AD 860: Æthelbald dies, and the crown passes to Æthelberht.

AD 865: Æthelberht dies, and the crown passes to Æthelred; the great heathen raiding army lands in Kent.

AD 866: York and the kingdom of Northumbria fall to the Vikings.

AD 868: Æthelred and Alfred march to besieged Nottingham; Alfred marries Ealswith.

AD 869: East Anglia falls to the Vikings; Edmund is martyred.

AD 871: Æthelred and Alfred fight the battle of Ashdown; Æthelred later dies, and the crown passes to Alfred.

AD 878: Guthrum invades Wessex; Alfred is driven into hiding in Athelney; Alfred fights the battle of Edington; Guthrum is baptized.

AD 885: Alfred drives the Vikings from the gates of Rochester.

AD 887: Alfred begins to read Latin.

AD 890: Guthrum, now Æthelstan, dies.

AD 892: Raiding army returns from the continent.

AD 896: Alfred's new longboats fight a sea-battle.

AD 899: Alfred dies, and the crown passes to Edward.

AD 924: Edward dies, and the crown passes to Æthelstan.

AD 937: Æthelstan is victorious at the battle of Brunanburh.

Introduction

This past year, while taking a moment between classes to relax in an Oxford common room, I began a conversation with an older English gentleman over a cup of tea. Noticing my American accent, he asked how I was getting on in England and if I had seen much of the beautiful countryside yet. I mentioned that I had hoped to take my family to Wantage that weekend because it had been the birthplace of Alfred the Great. He sipped his tea silently for a moment and then looked off into the distance with a skeptical eye and said,

"Alfred, hmmm. It's all very shrouded in myth, you know. I'm not sure if there actually was an Alfred."

You could tell that he was grappling with two problems. The first, I'm fairly certain, was a confusion between King Alfred and King Arthur. The second was a deep, deep need to express a scholarly dubiousness. This is the burden of the scholar, the need to scratch through the gilding that obscures the stories of history's heroes, to lay open the ugly truth of ulterior motives, vainglorious pride, and bad breath. But sometimes the heroes of history are truly worthy of the golden reputations they carry. Sometimes the truest retelling of the story is permeated with hero worship.

In the early, frigid months of AD 878, the whole of Britain had fallen to the savage dominion of the Viking invaders. The Saxon kings who had fought against the Danes had been either cut down in bloody combat or captured and executed in a gory sacrifice. A few lucky ones escaped the clutches of the Vikings and fled the island in humiliating defeat. Only one Anglo-Saxon king remained to hold off the Viking assault—King Alfred, the young king of Wessex. This is the story of the Anglo-Saxons' greatest king, the young man who, though driven from his throne and hunted everywhere by his savage enemies, refused to give up his fight for his nation.

This is the king who took a war-weary band of Anglo-Saxon men, hidden on the small swampy island of Athelney, and led them from where they teetered on the edge of extinction back to face their enemies once more on the battlefield. This is the man who later kindled such a flame for Christian learning in the hearts of his people that he launched the greatest literary renaissance that Anglo-Saxon England ever knew. This is the story of the only English king to be known as "the Great." He was a seasoned warrior, a scholar, a poet, a law-giver, an architect of towns and ships, and a zealous Christian.

Alfred was great because Alfred was a great king.

CHAPTER I

Holy Island

Behold the church of saint Cuthbert, splattered with
the blood of the priests of God, plundered of all its
treasures, a place more venerable than anywhere in
Britain is given over to pagan nations for pillaging . . .

—ALCUIN TO ETHELRED, KING OF NORTHUMBRIA

In the year *anno Domini* 937, Æthelstan, king of
the English people, stepped resolutely onto the
battlefield of Brunanburh, leading the might
of the Anglo-Saxon nation out to face the combined
forces of Vikings and Picts in what would be referred
to by successive generations
as "the great battle."[1] King
Æthelstan, grandson of Alfred
the Great, stood at the head
of the Saxon forces as they
heedlessly hurled themselves
at the spear-ready line of the

[1] The Vikings were
Scandinavian men
who traveled on
trading and raiding
expeditions mostly
in the North Atlantic
acquiring wealth for

their respective homelands in the territories known today as Denmark, Norway, and Sweden. It was the Danish Vikings, sometimes called the "Northmen," who were particularly active during the ninth and tenth centuries in the British Isles. Having already conquered the Picts in the area that would become Scotland a century later, the Vikings used the men as mercenaries against the Anglo-Saxons.

awaiting Danes and Picts. A thundering tumult the Saxons came, a reckless battering ram of mortal flesh, propelled by the passion and zeal of the king, whose fierce commands mounted up above the din and clamour of the chaotic charge. The linden shields of the Viking marauders split and shattered under the raging crush of the Saxon force. The Northmen faltered and staggered backward, yielding ground and, more importantly, leaving a number of gaps ripped through the center of their defensive wall.

With drawn swords and bloodcurdling yells, the Saxon warriors seized the opportunity and surged through the freshly torn gap in their enemies' wall. They poured through the defensive line, rent by their charge, like flood waters through a breeched dam, overpowering the stunned Vikings with sharp sword edge and cruel blunted hammer blows. The Norsemen and their Pict allies attempted to withdraw quickly in a desperate endeavour to regroup at a distance and make one more try at repelling the Anglo-Saxon assault. The tenacity and discipline of the Saxon troops had been carefully groomed over three successive generations of incessant battle against the pagan invaders. They left no room for retreat, no space for an orderly withdraw. Into the lines of the Vikings and the Picts they continued to surge, fighting fiercely, hewing down the astonished defenders with sword and axe.

The Viking shieldwall had been shattered; the nature of the combat shifted. Now the battlefield was no longer controlled by two large distinct armies. Instead it was bedlam, a chaotic quilt of thousands of small skirmishes with no rhyme or reason but rage and terror. On the warriors fought—man against man here, and two against one there. Soon the morning sun, God's bright candle, was looking down on the once green slopes of Brunanburh, now painted red with the blood of the fallen. Sensing the inevitability of their defeat, the entirety of the Viking army began to flee, running from the battlefield, wide-eyed and terror-stricken, abandoning the corpses of their fallen. But the Saxon press was unrelenting, and they pursued their vanquished foes hard across the countryside and into the surrounding woods.

By sunset, the Danes and the Picts had been entirely routed, and King Æthelstan, with his exhausted and bloodied troops, stood as the clear victor of the battle. This triumph made him the first Saxon king to be able to claim lordship over the whole of Britain, having driven the Vikings entirely from the island and having won the submission of the Picts and the Welsh. This battle also marked the end of a war against the Danish invaders that had begun many decades before Æthelstan's birth, a war that had been fiercely fought by Æthelstan's father, Edward, and his grandfather, Alfred.

And though Æthelstan was privileged to be the king standing victorious at that final battle, his great victory on the bloody fields of Brunanburh was only a small part of a much greater campaign waged by his predecessors. Æthelstan would be remembered for winning the "great battle," but his grandfather, Alfred, had set into

[2] At Alfred's birth, the island of Britain was divided into a number of different nations. In addition to the division between the Celtic tribes that ruled Scotland, Wales, and Cornwall, the area of modern-day England was divided up between a number of different Anglo-Saxon nations—Northumbria, Mercia, East Anglia, Wessex, and the several subkingdoms of Essex, Kent, Sussex, and others. Over the course of the reigns of Alfred, his son Edward, and his grandson Æthelstan, these various Anglo-Saxon kingdoms were gradually united into one great kingdom of the English people. And though we might anachronistically refer to the people Alfred ruled as the "English," this was a concept that was introduced by Alfred, halfway through his

motion the events that culminated in this victory, feats that ensured Alfred would always be remembered as the great king—Alfred the Great, king of Wessex.[2]

In the year AD 849, Osburh, the wife of Æthelwulf, king of Wessex (the Anglo-Saxon kingdom in the southwest of the island of Britain), gave birth to the king's fifth son during a stay at the small royal estate in the town of Wantage on the northern edge of the Wessex border. Alfred[3] was the last child born to Æthelwulf and Osburh, his oldest brother being more than twenty years older than him. With so many brothers between him and his father's crown, it was quite unlikely that Alfred would ever ascend to the throne of Wessex.

Alfred grew up roaming the countryside of Wessex alongside his father, who regularly journeyed throughout the many towns and cities within his kingdom. Sometimes on horse and sometimes on foot, Alfred learned the network of Wessex's old Roman roads, still used by the Anglo-Saxons. As they visited each city, Alfred's father and his advisors busied themselves with ensuring that the governing and taxation of the people had been competently managed. It was often a dull and dreary business. But the monotony of these bureaucratic chores was offset by the entertainments of the Saxon court.

There were the hunts, for which Alfred would have a particular fondness throughout his life. There were falconry, footraces, and horse races. There were wrestling, archery, sword fighting, and spear throwing. There were feasts with guests from afar—travelers, seafarers, experienced warriors, priests, traders, mercenaries, pagans, scholars, bishops, thieves, and princes. But most exciting of all, there were the poets. Alfred always had a particular fondness for the poetry of his native tongue. Late into the evenings, the Anglo-Saxon men would sit in the mead hall around a blazing fire, with their bellies full of roasted meat. The mead was poured out for each man from a gilded bull horn, and the enchanting thrumming of the scop[4] on his lyre began.

The songs Alfred heard in the mead hall as a boy intoxicated him. He was held in thrall by the stories of men charging grim-faced and stoic into battle. He was

reign. And it was not until the end of the reign of Æthelstan, and his victory at the battle of Brunanburh, that one could really speak of one English people.

[3] The four preceding sons had each been named with variations on their father's name—Æthelstan, Æthelbald, Æthelberht, and Æthelred. Even the Wessex king's one daughter, Æthelswith, carried this element in her name. The Anglo-Saxon word "Æthel" meant "princely" or "noble." But the "Æthel" element was dropped for his fifth son, Alfred, meaning "Elf wisdom."

[4] The Anglo-Saxon poet was called the scop, pronounced as "shope." He was the "shaper" or "creator." The poet was

the closest thing to God himself, who was the shaper of all of history. And the scop imitated the divine as he retold this history.

pierced by the lament of loss when lovers and lords were cut down by cruel blades or swallowed up by icy waves, and he quivered with a chilly awe when mortal men willingly sacrificed their lives for the sake of nobility and honor.

Alfred's mother offered a small book of poetry to the first of her sons who could commit the volume to memory. Though the book may have been small, the gift was a treasure—a small collection of Anglo-Saxon poems, carefully handwritten on pages cut from calfskin. The opening page was dazzling, with bright colors ornamenting the first letter of the first poem. Alfred, unable to read the book for himself, was fascinated by the beauty of the volume and jumped at the opportunity. He immediately took the book and found someone who could read the poems to him so that he could commit them to memory. Soon he returned, recited the entire contents of the volume, and collected his prize.

Lindisfarne Island lies off the northeast coast of England, just south of the Scottish border. It is a tidal island—when the tide is low, a narrow causeway connects Lindisfarne to the English coast, turning the island into a bulbous peninsula attached to the Northumbrian shore. But when the tide is high, the causeway is swallowed by the North Sea, and Lindisfarne becomes an island—the thousand-acre Holy Island. It is the epitome of seclusion: cold and grey, the air chilled by wind and wave-spray, filled with the cry of gulls and

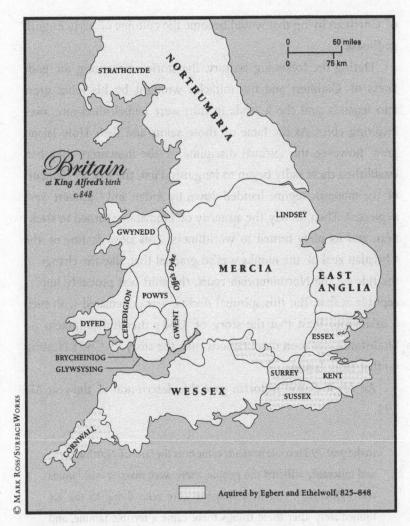

0 — 50 miles
0 — 75 km

STRATHCLYDE

NORTHUMBRIA

Britain
at King Alfred's birth
c.848

GWYNEDD

LINDSEY

Offa's Dyke

MERCIA

EAST
ANGLIA

CEREDIGION

POWYS

DYFED

GWENT

BRYCHEINIOG
GLYWYSING

ESSEX

SURREY

KENT

WESSEX

SUSSEX

CORNWALL

© MARK ROSS/SURFACEWORKS

Aquired by Egbert and Ethelwolf, 825–848

a palpable sensation of northernness. The island had been made
famous during the later half of the seventh century by the great
bishops Aidan and Cuthbert, whose austere piety had nurtured the
faith of the early Anglo-Saxon Christians and had set an example

of Christian living that would become the epitome of early English godliness.

During the following century, the stories recounting the godliness of Cuthbert and the miracles wrought by his relics grew into legends, and the legends in turn were embellished into awe-inspiring epics. As the fame of those saints and their Holy Island grew, however, the spiritual discipline of the monastery they had established there sadly began to languish. First, the stricter elements of the monastic regime handed down by Aidan and Cuthbert were neglected. Then, slowly, the austerity of Lindisfarne turned to slackness, and its piety turned to worldliness. This slow decline of the Christian zeal of the monks was so gradual that, like the change in the tide on the Northumbrian coast, the shift was probably imperceptible at first. But this spiritual decline was punctuated with such a calamitous blast that the story of God's dreadful judgment on Lindisfarne was soon more famous than the story of God's blessing on that Holy Island.

An Anglo-Saxon historian gave this description of the year AD 793:

In the year 793 terrible portents came over the land of Northumbria, and miserably afflicted the people, there were massive whirlwinds and lightenings, and fiery dragons were seen flying in the air. Immediately after these things there came a terrible famine, and then a little after that, six days before the Ides of January, the harrowing of heathen men miserably devastated the church of God on Lindisfarne, by plunder and slaughter.

—*Anglo-Saxon Chronicle*

For the historian who recounted these events, as he looked back on the year 793, it was easy to interpret the significance and import of these mysterious signs. Whirlwinds and lightning, famines and dragons[5]—all nature had been summoned as a portent for the coming judgment. The description of this particular Viking raid is rather brief and gives none of the details of the notorious sacking of Lindisfarne, but a good deal can be inferred from other Viking raids.

Lindisfarne was probably chosen as a target since churches and monastic communities offered the prospect of great wealth with very little protection. In the following years, monasteries throughout Britain and Ireland would fall prey to the Viking raids. The Vikings came from the sea, arriving in a handful of their longboats with little or no warning of their approach. Their shallow-drafted ships were beached on the shore of Holy Island and then pulled far enough up the shore to be safe from the tide for several hours. The monks, merely puzzled for the moment, watched from within the walls of the monastery. Then, once the ships were secured, the Vikings turned to the monastery.

It is unlikely that they met any resistance as they approached. No barrage of arrows and spears. No shieldwall. Not even an armed guard. After gaining an easy entrance, the raiding party plundered the monastery of whatever portable wealth could be found, hacking to pieces whatever feeble resistance the monks may have made.

[5] Contrary to many perceptions of this period in history, dragon stories were actually quite rare in Anglo-Saxon literature. The only significant account of a dragon to appear in the Old English stories was the story of the dragon in the poem *Beowolf*. And that dragon was not in England, but in Sweden.

Gold, silver, and jewels were seized and hauled back to the beached longboats, as well as any captives who might be sold on the slave market. They struck swiftly and ruthlessly, and then they quickly fled before any counterattack from a neighbouring village could be mounted. Throughout their time in Anglo-Saxon England, the secret to the Viking success would be the cunning selection of weak but wealthy targets and the hasty retreats, avoiding confrontation with the consistently slow-to-mobilize military forces.

Early descriptions of Viking attacks seized on the fact that Vikings made religious communities their targets of choice. According to the historians of the time, these marauding Northmen were pagan enemies of God, demonic forces at war with the Christian church. Some contemporary accounts describe the raiding Viking armies merely as "pagans" or "heathens." They coated the walls of the holy places with the blood of the saints and had no regard for the sacred things of the Christian church. Modern scholarship has felt burdened to counter this bias with an attempt toward a more impartial verdict. Now it is often pointed out that the Viking's selection of monasteries and churches for a prey was purely economic pragmatism. Christian churches simply provided the greatest possible gain at the lowest possible cost. The Viking attacks were driven not by a hatred of Christianity but by a cool and calculated evaluation of the Anglo-Saxon economy. So, considered from the perspective of the Northmen, who were not aware that the sacking of Christian holy places might be "taboo," these were perfectly viable targets.

It is unlikely, however, that the monks of Lindisfarne were unaware of this "other perspective." The role of the pagan raiding army had been played once before on the island of Britain when, several centuries before the Viking raiders, the Angles and the Saxons themselves had crossed the English Channel. Unconverted and bloodthirsty, these once-pagan tribes had abandoned their homes in modern northern Germany and Denmark in the fifth and sixth centuries and had crossed over to the isle of Britain preying upon the weaknesses of the natives who had been left vulnerable by retreating Roman troops.[6]

It was the establishment of the Christian church that turned the Anglo-Saxons away from a worldview that had been every bit as ruthless and cruel as the worldview held by the Viking raiders. The missionaries sent by Rome to Christianize the various warring Anglo-Saxon tribes had preached against and even given their lives in the fight against this very worldview.

Even after an Anglo-Saxon church had been firmly established, the English constantly had to fight the temptation to slip back into its own barbaric past, a godless past ruled by the worship of raw power. Threads of this old worldview remained woven throughout the poetry and songs of the Anglo-Saxons. There can be no doubt that when the Anglo-Saxon church named the Viking raiders *pagan*, they did not mean "people who have a different value system than we do." They meant *pagan* in

[6] From AD 43 until AD 410, England was under the control of the Roman Empire and known by the name *Britannia*. But as Rome became weakened by barbarian attacks through the end of the fourth century and into the beginning of the fifth, the Roman legions were pulled out of the island and returned to defend Rome. In the fifth century, migrating Anglo-Saxon tribes began to fill the power vacuum left by the Romans and, by the end of the sixth century, had conquered and settled the area that is now known as England.

its most proper sense: these raiding armies were full of warriors who acted like men without the gospel. It was a worldview known all too well to the men who named it as such, and it was a worldview they had rejected.

News of the sacking of Lindisfarne spread quickly. Alcuin, a native of Northumbria who was serving abroad in the court of Charlemagne, heard of the tragedy and wrote to Æthelred, king of Northumbria. In his letter, Alcuin took his inspiration from the prophets of the Old Testament who warned Israel to turn from her sins before God sent an even greater judgment.

> For nearly 350 years we and our fathers have dwelt in this most beautiful land, and never before has such a terror appeared in Britain, such as the one that we are suffering from this pagan nation. Nor was it thought that a ship would attempt such a thing. Behold the church of Saint Cuthbert, splattered with the blood of the priests of God, plundered of all its treasures, a place more venerable than anywhere in Britain is given over to pagan nations for pillaging . . . the heritage of the Lord has been given over to a people who are not his own. And where the praise of the Lord once was, now is only the games of the pagans. The holy feast has been turned into a lament.
>
> Carefully consider, brothers, and diligently note: lest this extraordinary and unheard of evil might be somehow merited by the habit of some unspoken wickedness. I am not saying that

the sin of fornication never appeared before among the people. But since the days of King Ælfwold, fornications, adulteries, and incest have inundated the land, such that these sins have been perpetrated without any shame, even against nuns who have been dedicated to God. What can I say about greed, robbery, and perverted judgments? When it is clearer than daylight, how much these crimes have flourished everywhere and it is witnessed by a plundered people.

Alcuin wrote a second letter to Higbald, the bishop of Lindisfarne. Again his letter sternly admonished the Christians of Lindisfarne that a disaster of this magnitude must be answered first and foremost with repentance, lest further catastrophe follow.

What confidence can there be for the churches of Britain, if Saint Cuthbert, with such a great number of saints, does not defend his own? Either this is the beginning of some much greater anguish or the sins of the inhabitants have demanded this. Clearly it has not happened by chance, but it is a sign that this was well deserved by someone. If there is anything that must be set right in your Grace's behavior, correct it swiftly.

But whatever response the Anglo-Saxons mounted, it was far too little and too late. The Vikings had tasted the undefended plenty of England and would soon return in greater and greater numbers. Rather than an unheard-of tragedy, "the church of Saint Cuthbert, spattered with the blood of the priests of God," would soon become an all-too-common scene throughout ninth-century Britain.

The year after the sacking of Lindisfarne, Vikings struck Jarrow, another monastic community farther down the coast, to the south of Lindisfarne. The next year Iona was plundered. And so on.

Initially the raiding parties consisted of small Viking bands traveling in as few as two to three ships, but occasionally parties came in larger fleets numbering as many as several dozen. The design of the Viking warship—perfected during the eighth century by northern sailors and shipwrights while transporting trade cargo along the Scandinavian coasts—played a significant role in the success of the raids. In the nineteenth century, the excavation of a burial mound on a Norwegian farm in Gokstad revealed the remains of a mid-ninth-century Viking ship, giving a likely example of the kind of vessel that prowled the Anglo-Saxon shores. The Gokstad ship has a length of seventy-six and a half feet and a width of seventeen and a half feet. The ship was clinker-built, meaning the hull was formed out

© MUSEUM OF CULTURAL HISTORY, UNIVERSITY OF OSLO, NORWAY / UNKNOWN PHOTOGRAPHER

of overlapping oak planks, joined with iron rivets and sealed with a caulking of tarred animal hair. Each layer of oak plank is called a *strake*, and the Gokstad ship was built of sixteen strakes. The nine lowest strakes would have been submerged when the ship was afloat. Though the draught of the ship was deep enough that the vessel could maintain a steady course in the heavy gales of the open seas as it sailed to Britain, the Gokstad ship would have generally required no more than a depth of three and a half feet of water to float freely. This meant that, in addition to being able to safely cross the North Sea loaded with plunder, the ship could be rowed up the shallow rivers that pierced deep into England's countryside without running aground. The fourteenth strake held sixteen oar holes per side, for a total complement of thirty-two oarsmen. Rowing would have been resorted to only occasionally, however, as the boat depended primarily on its sail for propulsion.

The men of the ninth-century Viking raiding party could leave their Scandinavian homes after the crops had been planted and the ice on the seas had melted. Then, traveling under the power of sails, their ships would reach the British shores within a matter of weeks. They could begin plundering along the coastline or could pierce deep into the heart of England, searching out the tributaries of the larger rivers like the Umber or Thames, switching to rowing when the winds failed. The Vikings would beach their ships just outside the walls of their target (rarely looking for targets very far from the waterways, which offered a hasty retreat). After striking their target and seizing whatever portable wealth could be found, they would then return to their ships and vanish, long before any force could be mustered to strike back. The Vikings then returned triumphant, laden down with booty and plunder, just in time to harvest their now fully grown crops.

Soon the stories of these horrific raids were reported throughout all of England. Every monastery and abbey, every marketplace, and every mead hall heard the haunting tales of the savage Viking attacks. Even Alfred, the young prince of Wessex, could not have been unaware of the nightmarish accounts of the pagan barbarians and their bloody raids. Nevertheless, Alfred's earliest years were relatively unaffected by the intermittent Viking raids. The story of the savage Northmen was just another thrilling feature of life growing up in the royal court of Wessex. More likely than not, the gory accounts of the Danish attacks added more to Alfred's daydreams than to his nightmares.

Alfred's biographer, a Welsh monk named Asser, later wrote that Alfred's parents had a particular fondness for him, an affection that exceeded their love for their other sons. Since Alfred was probably around twenty-five to twenty-six years younger than his oldest brother, this would imply that his mother, Osburh, was well into her forties when Alfred was born. At a time when the average person did not live past the age of thirty-two, Osburh must have felt like Sarah from the Bible: "old and well stricken in age, ceasing to be after the manner of women" (Genesis 18:11). It is quite likely that Alfred, the son of her old age, did hold a special place in the affections of his mother. His company was enjoyed enough that he was included in all the journeys of the royal court, a fairly exceptional practice at that time. The young boy's zeal for Anglo-Saxon poetry must have also endeared him to his mother.

In the year AD 853, at the age of four, Alfred was sent by his father on a lengthy pilgrimage from Wessex to Rome—the Holy City and the threshold of the apostles. Despite the prince's youth and the fact that he was fifth in line from the throne, Æthelwulf hoped the appearance of his young son in Rome would win the favor of the pope for the king and his nation. This trip must have had a lasting impact on Alfred, even at the age of four. The journey took the young boy across the English Channel, crossing from Canterbury to Calais.

In Calais was the beginning of a well-traveled path known as the *via francigena*. This route was formed by a series of connected roads leading pilgrims all the way to Rome, a road that Alfred's company most likely followed. This path broke the journey into some eighty stages, with each stage requiring a journey of approximately thirteen to fifteen miles. The trip was treacherous. Danes were raiding up and down the Frankish river systems, and Saracens had only recently been driven away from the gates of Rome. When travelers were not avoiding enslavement and slaughter at the hands of large pagan armies, they were running from smaller murderous bands of robbers who hunted the pilgrims' paths for easy wealth.

The route led all the way south through modern France, crossing the Alps in Switzerland, and then into Italy. Travelers along the *via francigena* stayed in a series of hostels, inns, churches, and monasteries, which had sprung up along the route to serve the needs of tired travelers. One of these small monastic communities in northern Italy ran a hostel in the town of Brescia. The monks of this particular monastery maintained a record of the various guests who had been given lodging in the hostel, a record preserved to this day with the scrawled signature "Alfred" among its ninth-century Anglo-Saxon guests.

After the several-months' journey of more than one thousand miles, Alfred and his noble company arrived in Rome, "the threshold of the apostles," a city of dazzling wealth, sophistication, and architecture far beyond anything Alfred had seen in Wessex. Here stood the Pantheon, the Coliseum, and countless other architectural relics of the Roman Empire, awe-inspiring even in their decay. But another Rome had risen out of those pagan ruins—the Christian city. And this city was still very much alive. Here Alfred could worship in the basilicas of Saint Peter or Saint Paul, both built over the graves of their respective apostles. Both basilicas rose more than one hundred feet and must have dwarfed any of the Anglo-Saxon buildings Alfred had ever seen. Saint Peter's Basilica had been the site of Charlemagne's crowning as emperor a little more than fifty years before.

But there was yet another Rome that must have caught Alfred's eye. Only ten years before Alfred's visit, Rome had been sacked by Saracen invaders who had plundered the city, including both the basilicas of Saint Peter and Saint Paul. As a result of this, Pope Leo IV had begun to refortify the city. The old city defenses had left the basilicas outside of the city's protective walls, making them easy targets for plundering. During the last Saracen invasion, the altar of Saint Peter's had been stripped of more than two hundred pounds of gold. Only a couple of years before Alfred's arrival, a new defensive wall had been completed, surrounding the city and providing protection for the vulnerable basilicas. This new wall marked off what would become known as the City of Leo, named for the pope who had constructed the new defenses. As the boy Alfred was shown through the city and the new city walls were pointed out to him, the day-dreams of fortifying a city against hostile invaders were planted in his imagination.[7]

Alfred's stay in Rome was brief. Once their task was accomplished and they had met Pope Leo IV, who confirmed him, tak-ing him as a spiritual son, the company of Anglo-Saxons was soon heading north, back up the *via francigena.*

[7] During their stay, the Anglo-Saxon pilgrims would have stayed in the *Schola Saxonum,* which lay just within the new defensive walls. The *Schola* had been established by an earlier king of Wessex, Ine, who had traveled to Rome over a century before to atone for his wicked reign. The *Schola Saxonum* was a large community of Anglo-Saxons living and working in Rome. It provided a hostel for Anglo-Saxon pilgrims and an Anglo-Saxon church, Saint Maria. The community of the *Schola* was large enough that during the recent Saracen assault on Rome, the Saxon troops mustered from the *Schola* constituted a significant portion of the city's defensive force.

By the year AD 854, Alfred had returned to Wessex and had suffered a terrible loss. Death had taken his oldest brother, Æthelstan, and his mother, Osburh. The death of his brother was not a significant blow for Alfred. Æthelstan was more than twenty years older than Alfred and had already been serving as a subking, in place of his father, over the kingdoms of Kent, Surrey, Sussex, and Essex. He had been absent for all of Alfred's life, so Alfred was not terribly attached to him. But the death of his mother, Osburh, must have shaken the boy Alfred profoundly.

At this time, Alfred's father, Æthelwulf, began to turn his mind to more eternal questions. The death of a son and of his wife, as well as his own advancing years, focused his thoughts on his mortality. As he considered his impending death, he was gripped by questions about the state of his soul. It was time to sort out a few things. During an Easter feast at the royal estate in Wilton, in AD 854, Æthelwulf announced a significant gift—an unprecedented royal tithe. In front of his four surviving sons, a handful of bishops and other churchmen, and a collection of his noblemen, the king of Wessex declared that he would give one-tenth of all his properties to the church "for the praise of God and his own eternal salvation." Then, spurred on by the stories that his youngest son had related, Æthelwulf announced his intentions to make a pilgrimage to Rome.

Æthelwulf made the necessary preparations for his journey and arranged for the governing of his kingdoms in his absence. Æthelbald, now the oldest of the sons, would rule Wessex. Æthelberht would rule the regions that Æthelstan, his now deceased older brother, had ruled as a subking—Kent, Surrey, Sussex, and Essex. It is not clear what role Æthelred, Æthelwulf's fourth son, played. But, as further proof of his favored status, Alfred was selected to stay by his father's side and to travel with his father on a pilgrimage to Rome, once again.

Once they entered the kingdom of West Francia, they were welcomed and entertained by the king of the West Franks, Charles the Bald. Charles also appointed a guide to lead them on the remainder of their trip, a monk named Markward, who accompanied them all the way to Rome. From Charles they passed to his brother, Emperor

Lothar, and from Lothar to Rome. Only a few months before their arrival in Rome, however, Pope Leo IV had died, and all of Rome had fallen into a bitter dispute about his legitimate successor. The clergy of Rome had appointed Benedict III, while the Carolingian Emperor Lothar had appointed a man named Anastasius. Alfred and Æthelwulf arrived in the midst of this ecclesiastical feud and the rioting that it inspired, although Benedict III was finally recognized as the legitimate pope shortly after their arrival.

This time, the party of Anglo-Saxon pilgrims stayed in Rome for an entire year. There were more than one hundred churches to visit and countless architectural feats to admire. And even though he was a young boy at the time of this visit, Alfred would still recall the buildings of Rome decades later and mention them in his writings. Æthelwulf, as king of Wessex, recognized his own particular responsibility for the *Schola Saxonum* and worked to restore the buildings that had been damaged in a recent fire. And, of course, Æthelwulf spent time paying his respects to the newly installed Benedict III.

The king of Wessex knew how to demonstrate his affections for the pope. He gave Benedict a golden crown weighing four pounds, bowls, beakers, various garments, and a beautiful sword crafted in the Anglo-Saxon style, with gold inlaid into the blade in a mesmerizing pattern. After presenting these gifts, Æthelwulf then went out and threw gold and silver coins to the crowds. This scene, the image of a king as a munificent gift-giver, became a foundational picture for Alfred of what true royalty looked like. It confirmed everything he had heard in the poetry of his native tongue about the importance of being a generous lord, a "ring-giver," as the poems would describe the legendary masters of old.

After the Anglo-Saxon royal party arrived back at the court of Charles the Bald in Verberie-sur-Oise, Æthelwulf announced his intention to take a new bride—Judith, Charles's twelve-year-old daughter. A marriage to the great-granddaughter of Charlemagne would ally Wessex with the most powerful family on the continent, shoring up his own authority and legitimacy throughout the Anglo-Saxon kingdoms of England.

Charles demanded that his daughter be received not only as the wife of Æthelwulf, but also as the queen of Wessex. Though it might seem to go without saying that the wife of the king would naturally be the queen, this was not the case in Anglo-Saxon Britain. Not since the infamous Queen Eadburh, wife of the Wessex king Beorhtric, had there been a queen of Wessex. Eadburh, in an attempt to control her husband, had worked to drive off the noblemen and advisors who surrounded him with her slanderous worm tongue. When defamation and gossip didn't work, she turned to murdering them with poison. One day she filled a poisonous cup for one of her intended victims and had it mistakenly given to her husband, King Beorhtric. After his death, Eadburh was driven from the kingdom.

The cautionary tale of Eadburh gave the later kings of Wessex cause for hesitation in crowning their wives as queen. Thus the kings of Wessex took wives but shared no royal authority with them and did not call them queens. The Wessex crown was meant to be passed on the "spear-side" and not on the "spindle-side," meaning the power was to be passed through male heirs and not through female heirs. But Charles insisted that Judith be anointed as queen, and Æthelwulf, desperate for the political alliance, consented.

From the raiding of Lindisfarne in AD 793 until well into the ninth century, the Viking raids continued to grow in intensity and regularity. Additionally, in the ninth century, the nature of the raiding parties began to shift. At first, a Viking band might be filled with an assortment of farmers and craftsmen—men who saw joining a raiding band as a two-month diversion from their regular work, a diversion that offered a bit of wealth and adventure. By the middle of the ninth century, however, the Viking ships were filled with professional warriors, men who considered plundering and pillaging as their life's calling. It is difficult to determine what caused this shift. Many suspect that the Scandinavian regions experienced a shortage of available farmland during this time due to either an overly abundant population (polygamy was common in Viking tribes) or changes in the weather patterns that rendered some of the Viking farmland unusable.

Regardless of the cause, the year AD 865 was setting up to be a formidable one for Alfred's father, King Æthelwulf, and his new bride.

CHAPTER 2

The Blood Eagle

Then King Edmund, the brave man that he was, said "I do not desire nor wish that I alone survive after my beloved thegns have been fiercely slain by these pirates in their beds, along with their children and wives. I never was the sort to take flight, and I would rather, if necessary, die for my own nation. God almighty knows that I will never falter from his service, nor from loving his truth. If I die, I live."

—FROM ÆLFRIC'S *Life of Saint Edmund*

In AD 865, a Viking army invaded Britain—an army unlike any of the preceding raiding bands, an army that was uninterested in quick plunder, an army set on long-term conquest. Three Viking brothers commanded this great army: Ivar the Boneless, Halfdan, and Ubbe. According to some later legends, these three warriors had come to avenge the death of their father, Ragnar Lothbrok (or Ragnar "Hairy Breeches"), who was said to have failed in an earlier invasion of Northumbria. The Northumbrian King Ælle had captured Ragnar and had him thrown into a pit of poisonous snakes. As Ragnar died, he cried out: "How the little pigs would grunt if they knew what was happening to the old boar!"

Before his failed attack on Northumbria, Ragnar had led a raiding party up the Seine River, into the heart of Charles the Bald's West Francia. Ragnar's Vikings encountered a minimal amount of resistance from the retreating Francian military as they plundered their way to Paris. The Francian forces retreated behind the fortified walls of monasteries, such as the monastery of Saint Denis, and watched in horror as the Vikings tortured and barbarically executed the captured Francian forces to the delight of the pagan raiding army. Ragnar and his men were eventually turned back, though it wasn't a fear of the Francian army that prompted the Viking's departure. Charles paid a hefty sum of seven thousand pounds in silver and gold to Ragnar, as *danegeld*, a bribe to convince the Vikings to leave. Usually the paying of the danegeld only guaranteed a much longer visit from the Danes, but at the same time that the payment was negotiated, the Viking forces were plagued by a severe epidemic of dysentery. The disease was so severe that Ragnar's forces were more than satisfied with the danegeld and immediately returned to their homes, hoping to recover in peace.

But they did not find peace at home. When Ragnar returned to Denmark, the king of the Danes, Horik, ordered all of Ragnar's forces to be executed as a punishment for their lawless raiding. Whether Horik was really bothered by the lawlessness of their raiding or by the competition that Ragnar's raiding posed to the crown is a question worth asking. Ragnar and his sons, however, managed to slip away from King Horik unharmed and began to focus their raiding away from the continent and onto the islands of Britain and Ireland.

Many years later, Ragnar's "little pigs" landed on the shores of East Anglia, on the southeast coast of modern England. The East Anglian king, King Edmund, quickly sought peace for his kingdom from the Vikings and found it could be purchased, though its cost would be far greater than Edmund bargained for. Ragnar's sons restrained their armies from pillaging the East Anglian kingdom, as long as the East Anglians supplied food and all other necessary provisions to the Viking camps, which began to swell daily with newcomers from other Viking armies hearing of this new life of ease. When the winter months arrived, a time when the Viking armies normally returned across the North Sea and left the Anglo-Saxon kingdoms to recover, the great army gave no hint of leaving.

Throughout the long winter, the East Anglians served the appetites of the Viking army, supplying them with food, drink, and other gifts. Then, in addition to these provisions, the Vikings demanded horses for the entire army. Though the Vikings never fought on horseback, they had learned that a mounted army had the ability to strike even deeper and more swiftly into the British countryside, where rivers did not always provide an easy path.

This last demand having been met, the Vikings finally marched on in the autumn of AD 866, leaving the East Anglians wishing they had been so lucky as to have only had their villages plundered and burned. From here, the great army, now more than five thousand strong, not counting the innumerable noncombatant members of their camp, rode north to the kingdom of Northumbria.

Whether there was truth to the legend of the death of Ragnar and the burden of revenge placed on his sons, or whether the wealth of the Northumbrian kings had caught their attention, the Danes were determined that their conquest of England was to begin with the Northumbrian capital of York.

The target was well selected. A commercial center that was advantageously connected to the network of roads and rivers of Northumbria, York offered quick wealth and a strategic base for further conquests. But even more strategic was the date chosen for the attack. First, Ivar and Halfdan arrived in Northumbria when the kingdom was divided by a cruel civil war between King Ælle and his rival, King Osberht. Second, the Vikings launched their surprise attack on York on November 1, All Saints' Day, a feast day the Anglo-Saxon church observed in great earnest. This meant that the attack came when the city was packed with the wealth of those who had come to observe the feast, as well as when the city was least prepared to defend itself because the two warring factions were absent from the city. And the city itself, busy with preparing for the feast, was entirely distracted from thinking of its own defenses.

Undefended, York quickly fell to the Viking attack. Upon hearing the news, Ælle and Osberht, recognizing how dire the situation was, quickly made peace with each other, joined their forces into one large Anglo-Saxon army, and returned to prepare for their own assault on the now Viking-held York. Their attack came several months later, on March 23, Palm Sunday. Initially the battle favored the Northumbrian forces, who broke through the walls of York and engaged the Viking warriors on the narrow streets of the city. But the tide of the battle suddenly turned, and the forces of Ælle and Osberht were cut down both inside the city walls and outside as they fled.

Though both Ælle and Osberht fell that day, the death of Ælle would be particularly immortalized by later Viking sagas, eager to emphasize the revenge Ragnar's sons were able to exact from the man who had executed their father. Ivar and Halfdan captured Ælle and ordered him to be ritually sacrificed to the Norse god Odin, the Viking war god who had given the victory to the Norse raiders. The particular method of sacrifice chosen for Ælle was the grisly ceremony of the Blood Eagle. Ælle was held face down on the ground while a sword chopped two gaping holes into the back of his ribcage, one on each side of his spine. Then to the cheers of the Vikings crowded around the floundering victim, his ribs were pulled back and his still-inflating lungs were seized and pulled out through the bloody holes, heaving and gurgling through the last few painful gasps of the shrieking sacrifice.[1]

[1] The Vikings took comedic delight in their cruelties. In one Icelandic saga, the Viking warrior Egill is captured by the owner of a farm he is trying to plunder. In the middle of the night, Egill and his men get free from their bonds and plunder the farmer's belongings once more. However, as they sneak back to the ship, Egill begins to feel a tinge of guilt for his theft, realizing he has acted as a thief and not a warrior. And so, Egill sneaks back to the farm and lights it on fire, burning its inhabitants in their beds and turning himself into an honorable warrior. The crueler the death, the more enjoyable the story. No doubt, the retelling of Ælle clawing the ground as the sword hacked at his rib cage provided innumerable delights around Viking campfires for many of the following decades.

Shortly after Æthelwulf married Judith, but before the royal family returned to Wessex, Alfred's brother,

Prince Æthelbald, had attempted to usurp the throne. The prince had announced that he refused to let his father back into Wessex and intended to rule as king in his place. Æthelwulf apparently did not take much notice of this attempted coup and returned to Wessex. Æthelbald, his bluff called, was given several shires in the west of Wessex to rule in exchange for his peaceful submission to his father.

With his mother, Osburh, dead and his father more and more distracted, Alfred found it increasingly easier to slip through the cracks in his father's courts. Though he maintained the fondness for Anglo-Saxon poetry his mother had instilled in him, far less effort was put into his studies. In fact, it was not until the age of twelve that Alfred learned to read in his native tongue, but he was still not able to understand anything in Latin, the language in which most literary works of the time were available.

In January 858, within two years of his return home, King Æthelwulf died, leaving the throne to his grasping son Æthelbald. Unfortunately, Æthelbald was not satisfied with just the throne. Shortly after he was made king of Wessex, Æthelbald took his step-mother, the fourteen-year-old Queen Judith, as his wife. Thinking that his marriage to Judith would bring all the Carolingian legitimacy that his father had received from having married the girl, Æthelbald was surprised to find that he had merely invoked disgust and not respect in the hearts of his subjects. Taking his father's bride for his own wife was a violation of canon law and nature itself. The rash move could have endangered his reign had he not died of disease not long after the wedding. Judith soon returned to her father in West Francia, and the power of Wessex was once again reserved for the spear-side.

After the death of Æthelbald in AD 860, Æthelberht, the

next son in line, took the throne. Æthelberht now ruled over all of Wessex, as well as the northern shire of Berkshire, and the eastern subkingdoms of Kent, Surrey, Sussex, and Essex. But as was his older brother's, Æthelberht's reign was brief. By AD 865, Æthelberht was dead as well, leaving the fourth son, Æthelred, as king and Alfred as the next in line.

With the conquest of the Northumbrian capital of York, Danish rule had been thoroughly established in the north, and it was time for the Viking forces to begin expanding their empire. In AD 867 Ivar and Ubbe led the army south to Nottingham—the capital of the kingdom of Mercia, the northern neighbors of Wessex.[2] The city was quickly captured by the Viking army, who refortified it against any attempts to retake the city. The Mercian king, Burgred, appealed to Wessex for aid in ending the Danish occupation of Nottingham. The Mercian kingdom was closely allied to Wessex after King Æthelwulf's daughter, Æthelswith, married the king of Mercia in the spring of 853 in an attempt to forge a military alliance between these two kingdoms. Thus Burgred and the new king of Wessex, Æthelred, were brothers-in-law.

Æthelred quickly consented and set about raising the army of Wessex to go and battle the Danish invaders.

[2] At that time, more than three centuries before the time of Robin Hood, the Anglo-Saxon name of Nottingham was *Snotengaham*, apparently named after an earlier chieftain named Snot. Luckily for the modern-day residents of the city, the "S" was eventually dropped from the name, and so, rather than Snottingham, the city is now called Nottingham.

When Æthelred and his younger brother Alfred finally arrived at Nottingham leading the battle-ready men of Wessex, however, they were frustrated to find that the Danes had withdrawn behind the city walls of Nottingham and refused to come out and fight. Many years of raiding and running had taught the Viking forces the advantage of avoiding all combat except when they were sure to be the victors. And now, even though the goal of the Vikings was no longer simply plundering but all-out conquest, they continued to use many of these old tactics.

The forces of Wessex were not prepared to break through Nottingham's old Roman ramparts and its city walls. They had no choice but to settle in for a lengthy siege of the city. Unfortunately, unlike Ivar and Ubbe's army, the men of Wessex were not professional soldiers. This meant that though they could be counted on for fierce fighting during short and intense battles, they could not be counted on for long, protracted campaigns. These men were farmers who had to return home to tend to their crops and livestock and could not spare months of waiting for the Viking troops to be starved into submission by a dwindling food supply. After a very short time, the Wessex forces began to steal out of the camp secretly in order to return home. Burgred, realizing he would not be able to wait the Vikings out, reluctantly won peace for his city by bribing the raiding army to leave.

This was Alfred's disappointing introduction to the bitter frustration of doing battle with the Viking raiders. Though the reputation of the Danes for ferocity in battle was well deserved, the true skill of the Viking forces was the ability to maximize their raping, pillaging, and plundering, while minimizing the chances of facing another army on the open field of battle. Ivar and Ubbe led their troops past Æthelred, Alfred, and Burgred, completely unscathed, with the plundered wealth of the city on their backs. The Mercian king, Burgred, though he had won back the city, had ultimately lost his authority to rule. During the following years, the kingdom of Mercia became a thoroughfare for Viking armies, with the Mercians incapable of putting up any resistance.

Alfred did find one rather significant consolation in the failed siege of Nottingham. At some point during, or shortly after, the siege, Alfred was betrothed to and then married a Mercian woman, Ealswith. His new bride's father was an ealdorman of one of the older tribes of Mercia, and her mother was from the royal line of the Mercian kingdom. She remained married to Alfred for the rest of his life, dying several years after her husband.

Though Alfred said little about his relationship with his wife in his writings, his silence is in keeping with the general Anglo-Saxon austerity and does not indicate any particular coolness on Alfred's part toward his wife. The notions of chivalric romance and knights sick with love for beautiful maidens would not come to England for another several hundred years. Not until long after Norman rulers from northern Europe replaced the Anglo-Saxon kings would the idea of romantic love become a prominent theme in English literature. Therefore Alfred's silence about his marriage can't be interpreted as indifference to Ealswith. Like all Anglo-Saxon men, he did not wish to share with the world his romantic affections for his wife.

Their marriage was a fruitful one, with Ealswith giving Alfred two sons and three daughters (in addition to other children who did not survive into adulthood).

There is one story about his wedding, however. As Alfred moved from boyhood to manhood and the passions and lusts of a young man began to grip him, he became alarmed at the sudden power of these new temptations. Fearing the bondage of these lusts and the possibility of losing favor with God if he gave in to them, Alfred began the habit of going to churches very early in the morning to beg God that he might send him some sort of physical affliction that would be severe enough to curb his sinful lusts, but not so severe that it would render Alfred useless in his duties. God seemingly answered Alfred's prayers by afflicting the prince with the extremely unpleasant disease of piles. Alfred suffered from this malady for years, and after some time the affliction became more than he could take.

Finally, exhausted by the pain and humiliation of his disease, Alfred prayed again that God might replace his disease with something less painful and less grotesque. After this prayer, Alfred never suffered from piles again. On the day of his marriage to Ealswith, in the middle of the marriage feast, however, a severe and incapacitating pain struck Alfred. The affliction of piles had been replaced by a mysterious internal agony. This pain would continue to recur for the next twenty years of Alfred's life, leaving him in constant fear of its onset.

In the year AD 869, the Viking army poured from York to the south once more. Marching through Mercia, which now made no attempt to stop them, the pagan army advanced on East Anglia, the site of their initial landing in Britain five years earlier. The East Anglian king, Edmund, had fed the Viking forces for an entire year and then supplied enough horses for the entire army's journey to York. Now the Vikings came to repay this favor by conquering the East Anglian kingdom entirely.

The East Anglian army, unprepared for the surprise attack, was beaten easily. On November 20, 869, Edmund was taken captive by the Viking chieftains Ivar and Ubbe and, according to the story passed on by his sword-bearer, was tortured and executed. First the king was bound to a tree, where he was scourged and beaten. Then the Vikings shot arrows at him until he "bristled like a hedgehog." Annoyed at his continued calling out to Christ, the Vikings finally beheaded him.

And so, with Northumbria conquered and the kingdoms of Mercia and East Anglia crippled, the only Anglo-Saxon nation left to be subdued by the raiding Vikings was the kingdom of Wessex.

Chapter 3

The Battle of Ashdown

When Alfred could no longer hold off the enemy
battle line, without either retreating back from the
fight or prematurely charging against the enemy troops
before his brother had come to the battle, he finally
commanded the Christian troops to advance against
the enemy army, acting manfully, like a wild boar.

—From Asser's *Life of Alfred*

After conquering East Anglia, the Viking
army was slightly reorganized. Ivar the
Boneless returned to York, now called by
its Viking name *Jorvik* and functioning as the capital
of the Viking-controlled north. Ivar soon traveled to
Dublin where he was later killed. Ubbe also departed
to inflict himself upon the Welsh, leaving the Danish
forces to be led by Halfdan and Bagsecg, another
Viking king who had only recently arrived in Britain
to add his forces to the swelling Viking hordes.
Having settled in the East Anglian town of Thanet,
they continued to raid and plunder the East Anglian

countryside. But even as the air turned bitter cold with the oncoming winter, the Viking chieftains began to gather supplies and make all the necessary preparations for their armies to move out once more.

By December 870, the Danish forces were ready. Despite the treacherously worsening weather of the winter months, they boarded their longships and set out to sea, working their way down the eastern coast, all the way to the mouth of the Thames. Then, turning up into the river, alternating between rowing and sailing, they followed the snaking waters deep into the heart of Britain. Their destination was the last defiant Saxon kingdom—Wessex. As Halfdan and Bagsecg moved their massive fleet silently up the Thames, a portion of their forces must have traveled over land. How they managed to keep the news of their movement completely silent is difficult to explain. By the opening days of the year 871, the various components of the Viking forces had reunited and were crouching on the very borders of Wessex.

The first assault was swift and successful. In a few hours, the Viking raiders attacked and quickly captured the unsuspecting and unprepared town of Reading. Reading lay in the center of Berkshire, a county the Mercians had ceded to Wessex only a few decades earlier. The town was strategically located at the confluence of the river Thames and the river Kennet, providing natural defenses as well as mobility for the Viking longships. But it was also conveniently placed very near several attractive targets for Viking pillagers—the abbey of Abingdon and the royal estate of Wallingford (not to mention the royal estate already located in Reading). Immediately after seizing Reading, the Vikings began constructing an earthen rampart that spanned the distance between the two rivers and left the Vikings in a well-protected triangular stronghold, surrounded by rivers on two sides and an easily defended rampart on the third.

As these defenses were being constructed, two Viking earls rode out with a raiding band intent on looting some of the nearby farms to begin providing for the Vikings' voracious appetites, as well as to begin familiarizing themselves with the area surrounding their new fortress. As they explored their environs, however, these two Viking earls discovered that news of their arrival in Wessex had traveled quickly. Twelve miles from Reading, near a small village called Englefield, the reconnoiter of the Wessex countryside was interrupted by an ealdorman of Berkshire named Æthelwulf and a host of men whom he had marshaled for battle. Too far from their newly constructed defenses of Reading and cut off from their fellow Danish troops, the Viking party was forced to stand and fight the troops of Wessex.

The struggle between the two forces was protracted and savage. Although it was true that the Viking strategy generally was to avoid having to step onto the battlefield with a prepared army, that should in no way give the impression that the Viking forces were incapable of fierce fighting. Once it was clear that the Vikings could not simply withdraw and wait for the Berkshire ealdorman to pay for his peace, the Danish forces eagerly and zealously turned themselves to the ugly business of hacking their way through the men of Berkshire.

Their hopes of easily returning to the secure outpost in Reading were soon dashed when they realized the men of Berkshire were not so easily conquered. Ealdorman Æthelwulf was an experienced warrior. Ten years before, when a Viking navy had attempted an attack on the city of Winchester, it was Ealdorman Æthelwulf, leading the men of Berkshire, who had driven the Danish raiders from the city. Æthelwulf and his men showed the same resolve once more.

Again and again the Vikings threw themselves at the line of Saxon shields, and each time the Saxon men, grim and determined, matched and bettered the Vikings' power, defiantly driving them back. Despite the Danish ferocity, the Saxon men just wouldn't back down. Even worse, they gained ground on the Viking army. After one of these engagements, when it was discovered that the Saxons had cut down Sidroc, one of the two Viking earls, the raiding army began to lose its resolve. Soon panic struck the Danish troops, who were far more accustomed to seeing fear in the eyes of their opponents than in the eyes of their comrades.

Panic then gave way to a frenzied horror, and soon the somewhat astonished Berkshire troop stood victorious as the masters of the battlefield as the Vikings ran from the slaughter.

Æthelwulf was soon able to report the news of his glorious victory in person to Æthelred, the king of Wessex, and his younger brother Alfred. The royal brothers arrived in Berkshire soon after Æthelwulf's encounter with the raiding band. Within four days of the Berkshire forces' encounter with the Danish army, Æthelred and Alfred had gathered the Wessex military before the earthen ramparts of Reading and prepared their men for an assault on the Viking stronghold.

Unlike Æthelwulf, this would be the first actual combat that either Æthelred or Alfred had ever faced. The closest the two brothers had come to real fighting had been during the siege of Nottingham—a siege that had been resolved with the payment of the danegeld rather than with the sword point. Now Æthelred, twenty-five, and Alfred, twenty-two, arranged the might of Wessex for an assault on the Viking defenses, a daunting task.

In almost any combat engagement, it is understood that defensive forces command a significant advantage over the attacking troops. A soldier carefully selects and prepares his defensive position to guarantee that it affords him the most cover while forcing his enemy to approach him as vulnerably as possible. And though this is generally understood by all armies, it was particularly well understood by the Viking forces. Throughout the ninth century in northern Europe and the islands of Ireland and Britain, the Vikings had perfected the art of digging in and forcing their opponents to make enormous sacrifices in every assault on a Danish position. All of this is to say that the assault on Reading did not go well for Wessex's forces, and the introduction to combat given to Æthelred and Alfred was not a pleasant one.

Initially the Wessex attack caught the Viking forces by surprise. Æthelred, Alfred, and Æthelwulf, shoulder to shoulder with their troops, swooped down on Reading, hacking and hewing their way through the startled resistance. But by the time the Saxons had pushed the Vikings back to the walls of the fortress, the gates opened, and an inexorable tidal wave of Danish warriors poured forth, driving the men of Wessex back and crushing their hopes of a victory. Later descriptions of the battle claimed the Vikings had poured out of the gates like wolves hungry for battle. Soon the men of Wessex had turned and fled. For miles the Vikings pursued the fleeing Saxons. It was not until the Saxon troops crossed the river Loddon at a hidden ford that the Vikings finally gave up the chase and Æthelred and Alfred had a moment to compose themselves and their troops. The fight had been humiliatingly lost, and Æthelwulf, their most experienced military commander, was dead.

Æthelred and Alfred were struck with grief and shame at their terrible defeat. Their first attempt at combat had been a dismal failure costing countless lives, including one of Wessex's most seasoned military leaders, and leaving the rest of Wessex vulnerable to a Viking attack. Though the loss had been significant, it was of the utmost importance that Wessex's forces regroup and the zeal of the soldiers be rekindled. The poor performance in the assault on Reading and the subsequent hasty retreat had communicated to the Vikings the weakness of the Wessex troops and the vulnerability of their cities. The Danes were sure to follow up on their victory with an assault on other towns in Wessex. The Saxons had to reorganize swiftly and prepare to meet this inevitable attack.

There was no hope of aid from Northumbria, East Anglia, or Mercia. All the other Anglo-Saxon kingdoms had either been conquered or were so entirely intimidated by the Danish armies that coming to the aid of Wessex was out of the question, leaving Wessex to stand alone. As the Vikings advanced into the heart of Wessex, intending to ravage the land as they had throughout Northumbria and East Anglia, the men of Wessex were left with little choice. They rushed to cut off the Viking advance, intercepting the Danish raiders at Ashdown, where they were able to force the Vikings to face them in battle.

Since Ashdown was not the name of a specific point, but rather a general term for the entire stretch of the Berkshire downs, the exact location of the battlefield is a puzzle to modern historians. The clues given by the ninth-century accounts of Alfred's movements are difficult to interpret with any degree of certainty. Asser, Alfred's friend and biographer, recorded that the Latin name for Ashdown was *mons fraxini*, or "the hill of the ash." But the only landmark identified by Asser was a small and solitary thorn tree around which the battle raged. That lonely thorn tree must have etched itself on the memories of the Ashdown veterans, since Asser took the time to mention in his brief description of the battle how he had seen that very thorn tree.

The prevailing theory that the battle of Ashdown happened at Kingstanding Hill, not far from the village of Moulsford on the

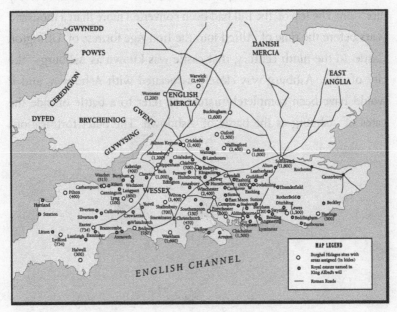

© MARK ROSS/SURFACEWORKS

banks of the Thames, is incredibly speculative. The theory is based on the assumption that the Vikings, after having successfully held off the forces of Wessex at Reading, *may* have immediately turned their attentions north to the military stronghold at Wallingford and the riches of the wealthy abbey at Abingdon. If the Vikings had done so, then a strategic position for repulsing the Viking attack *might* have been Kingstanding Hill. And though this is all plausible, it rests on a series of guesses with no actual historical evidence to back up the speculation.

The most popular traditional account identifies Ashdown with what is now known as Whitehorse Hill, an imposing hill that looms over the low-lying Berkshire Downs. It stands around nine hundred feet above sea level, making it the tallest point from miles in every direction. The top of the hill had been converted more than a thousand years before the time of Alfred into the Iron Age fortress of Uffington Castle. In the ninth century, that castle was known as Ashburg—the city of Ash. Ashburg was closely associated with Ashdown, and it would have been completely natural to refer to a battle outside the gates of Ashburg as the battle of Ashdown. The outer fortifications

would have provided an imposing defensive wall for the raiding army. The height of the hill supplies a commanding view in all directions, making it an ideal position from which the Viking camp could have easily watched for the approaching Wessex army.

Carved into the turf of the northwest slope of the hill, near its summit, is the mysterious chalk outline of a galloping white horse. The charging horse, in its perpetual career, stretches almost four hundred feet along the top of the steepest slope of the hill. Ancient artists first dug a maze of trenches across the hillside and then filled the trenches with chalk rubble in order to trace the white figure into the hillside. Though the earliest reference to the white horse comes from the eleventh century AD, modern dating techniques have suggested that the horse could have been cut into the hillside as early as 1000 BC. No clear account of the horse, who made it, or why it was made can be given.

The white horse has gathered many of the myths of history to itself, and those myths have grown more and more fantastical grazing on the green slopes of the vale. King Arthur, Saint George, and Alfred the Great are all claimed by the white horse, and the region surrounding the hillside is littered with the relics of their legends. Arthur's father, Uther Pendragon, is said to have fought a victorious battle in the valley below. One story claims that Whitehorse Hill is actually Badon Hill, the site of one of Arthur's great victories.

The Norse god of blacksmithing, Wayland, is said to have manned his forge a mile from Whitehorse Hill at Wayland's Smithy, a Neolithic barrow. Some stories have Wayland himself forging Arthur's great sword, Excalibur. Some say that, once a year, the white horse leaves the hillside and walks down to the valley below (known as the "manger") to graze. But others insist that the white horse won't leave the hillside until King Arthur returns. And then he won't just graze in the manger; he will dance along the Berkshire Downs to welcome the king home.

Other legends insist that the carving on Whitehorse Hill does not depict a horse at all, but rather a dragon—Saint George's dragon. One historian claimed that the conspicuous little knob bulging out of the valley below Whitehorse Hill is the very spot where Saint George killed his dragon. The poisonous blood of the slain dragon spilled out on the top of the hill, burning a bare patch into the ground where the dragon lay—a bare patch that endures to this day. The association with Saint George's dragon is so strong that the hill is now known simply as "Dragon Hill." However, some deny that George killed his dragon on the mountain. They insist that the strange mound *is* the dragon, or more precisely, his burial mound.[1]

Alfred's own story is not without embellishment. According to one legend, Alfred gathered the men of Wessex to the battle of Ashdown by using the ghostly blast of the blowing stone, a peculiar hunk of sarsen stone that was found on the top of a nearby hill. The stone stands around three feet high and is pierced throughout by a maze of holes, some going only a few inches and stopping and some threading all the way through the stone via a network of winding chambers and chasms. The stone now sits in the front yard of a cottage not far from Blowing Stone Hill, where it once sat. The hole that serves as a mouthpiece is found

[1] The strange little mountain looks out of place in the valley, but modern descriptions of Dragon Hill always begin with the assertion that "it is a completely natural formation and not man-made."

on top of the stone, its rim polished by centuries of lips pressing it smooth. Passersby are still welcome to give the stone a toot. The occupant of the cottage, I imagine, could be identified by a jittery, haunted aspect and poor hearing.

The numerous fantastical elements attributed to Whitehorse Hill have had the effect of making the whole setting seem too mystical to be true. It has become the sort of setting that scholars tend to wave their hands at and say, "It's all shrouded in myth. We're not even sure if there ever really was a Whitehorse Hill." But there is the horse, ghostly white and galloping along the hillside, whether or not we believe in his countless legends. We know that there really was an Alfred, who stood and faced the Viking invaders on the battlefield in AD 871. And though we may not know for certain that Whitehorse Hill was the site of the battle, it is easily the most likely candidate.

When Alfred composed his will many years later, he left three of his fifty-five estates to his wife Ealswith. One was Wantage, the place of his birth. The other two were Edington and Lambourn. Edington was the site of one of Alfred's later victories over Viking forces. Lambourn was an estate just south of Whitehorse Hill, the site where, according to legend, Alfred gathered his forces just before the battle of Ashdown. It would seem that when Alfred composed his will, he picked three properties filled with personal significance to give to his wife. Last, it should be remembered that the only identifying feature the historian Asser gave for the battlefield of Ashdown was a solitary thorn tree. Oddly, the Anglo-Saxon charter describing the Whitehorse hillside named a solitary thorn tree as one of the identifying features of the property line.

Though these clues may not form definitive proof that

Whitehorse Hill was the site of the battle of Ashdown, they present a much stronger case than any of the other proposed locations. One certainly begins to wonder what caused scholars to become so sensitive about the legend of the white horse and forced them to prefer other more speculative options. Virtually the only thing that makes Kingstanding Hill more preferable than Whitehorse Hill is that it is not legendary.

Kingstanding Hill is not smothered with legends and has a non-mythical, unromanticized, scholarly plainness about it. It can be slipped into a footnote without attracting attention to itself, whereas the Whitehorse immediately evokes snorts and guffaws because of the preposterously fantastical legends heaped onto it. But this is such a remarkably miserly way to interpret the evidence. It is more likely that the many layers of legends surrounding Whitehorse Hill have

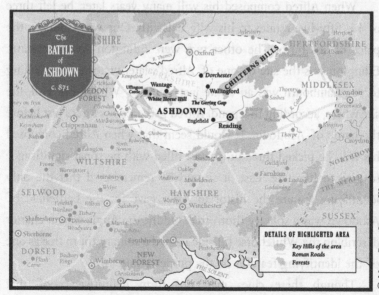

accumulated there because, as the location of the great battle of Ashdown, it was assumed that other spectacular events must have happened there as well.

The Viking forces carefully chose their battle positions before the soldiers of Wessex had arrived at Ashdown. Bagsecg and Halfdan, the two Viking kings, selected the highest point on the hillside for their defensive position, lining up their men along the crest of the ridge and forcing the Wessex army to attack from below. Though the Vikings may have been using horses or ponies to speed their travel, the horses would have been released before the battle because the Vikings preferred to fight on their feet rather than on horseback. The Danish army was then divided into two units—one commanded by the two Viking kings, Bagsecg and Halfdan, and the other commanded by a collection of the Viking earls.

Though the Vikings, as a result of cunning and not cowardice, may have frequently used a strategy that minimized engaging in the sort of open-field combat they were about to face the Viking soldiers were nothing but battle hungry on that bitterly cold morning. Like hungry wolves, they waited uneasy, almost parched with blood thirst. They sat on the ridge, watching for the approach of the Wessex soldiers from below, testing their blades and tightening their armor, promising their gods a grisly sacrifice of victims soon to be offered up on the battlefield.

The tools of the trade, the weapons of the Viking warrior, played such a significant role that they were often prescribed by

Danish law and were regularly inspected by legal officials to ensure that each and every free Viking male was prepared to play the important role of warrior. Each soldier was required to carry a sword or a battle-axe, a shield, and a spear. Swords tended to be the weapons of the wealthier Viking warriors. The sword blade was generally around two-and-a-half to three-feet long, double-edged, and constructed to be held in one hand. Since swords were already significantly more expensive than axes, they tended to be more ornate. The hilt of the sword was often elaborately decorated with costly metals, figures, and patterns. Some were marked with runic letters, engraved into the blade, which either named the blade or invoked magical powers to give the blade bloody success in battle.

The less wealthy of the Viking warriors, who could not afford a sword, settled for an axe. Most of these axes were everyday tools and were not reserved solely for battle. They were not double-edged, contrary to many modern depictions. They were single-edged blades, measuring anywhere from three to seventeen inches across the arc of the blade. The haft on which the axe head sat was anywhere from twenty to forty inches long. The shorter the handle, the easier the axe would have been to wield with one hand, leaving another hand free to hold a shield, and the easier to throw as well. Longer-handled axes required two hands for swinging, so the soldier lost the ability to use a shield but added great force and reach to the deadly chop.

The Viking shield was circular, two and a half to three feet in diameter. The bulk of the shield was constructed of wooden planks, less than half of an inch thick, butted together, bound together by metal bands, and covered in leather. At the center of the shield was a large hole in the wood, covered by a six-inch iron dome called the "shield boss." Inside the boss a handle was mounted for gripping the shield. The protection offered by the wooden planks of the outer shield was not much use in close hand-to-hand fighting since a few blows of an enemy sword or axe would cut it to kindling. The usefulness of the shield was the protection it offered from the attack of arrows and spears fired as the opposing forces were still closing in on one another. Though the missiles pierced the wooden planks slightly, the shield offered adequate protection from the barrage.

The shield boss ensured that the point where the Viking gripped his shield was entirely protected, keeping his shield hand safe from harm. The shield boss also offered a second offensive weapon once the clash of close combat had begun. Though the wooden shield would be slowly chopped away in the hand-to-hand hacking, the large iron dome gripped in the fist of the shield hand became a deadly cudgel delivered in the form of a left hook.

Lastly, each man carried his spear. Though the modern audience tends to think of the spear as a clumsy accessory and not as crucial to the warrior's arsenal as the sword or shield, this opinion was not shared by the ninth-century Viking. Once two forces had closed on each other, the spear was often the most effective tool for reaching past the enemies' defenses and striking a lethal blow. The iron spearhead was anywhere from eight inches to two feet in length. It was crafted with a savage beauty, lethally barbed and inlayed with intricate designs in precious metals. The shaft of the spear, cut from the wood of the ash tree, could reach up to ten feet in length. The spears were carefully balanced so that they could be thrown with a deadly accuracy. In open battle, however, most spears were held, rather than thrown, and used for thrusting once the two armies clashed.

Armor, like the sword, was expensive and therefore available only to those who paid handsomely. It would be possible but rare to find a Viking in a mail "byrnie," a large mail shirt. The Viking helmet with its iconic horns, ever-present in modern depictions of the Viking warrior, is almost entirely a fantasy. Occasionally a particularly wealthy Danish chieftain might be found in an iron helmet with an ornamented ridge arcing over the top of the skull, for added protection, and an extravagant faceguard, crafted more with an eye toward terrifying the enemy than actually protecting the face. But the horns are a myth and never appeared on the Viking helmet.

The Viking forces lined up on the winter-chilled slope of Ashdown and stood proudly waiting for the troops of Wessex to make their way up the hillside. The division of the Viking army into two units had been communicated to King Æthelred and his brother Alfred earlier in the morning, while they were still in their camps a short distance from the battle. The two decided on a course of action similar to the strategy of the Danish army. Æthelred would take half of the troops and face the two Viking kings—Bagsecg and Halfdan. It was only appropriate that the Wessex king face off against the Viking kings. Alfred would take the second half of the Wessex army and take his stand against the Viking earls and their warriors. This battle plan having been fixed, the two brothers said their good-byes to one another and returned to their troops to face their fortunes in war.

As he returned to his men, Alfred was faced with a difficult task. He was barely twenty-two years old and had only experienced his first combat four days earlier, an experience that had not gone well for him or his troops. He was neither a king nor a seasoned warrior. He had little to commend himself to the men of Wessex who were now expected to follow him up the soon-to-be-bloodied slope of Ashdown. Lacking age, experience, and the crown, Alfred had no room for indecision, bumbling, or cowardice. His demeanor had to be resolute, sharp, and bold.

After he had returned to his men, he wasted little time before informing them of the task at hand. He charged them to acquit themselves like men, to be worthy of the king they served, to remember their God, and to trust in God's strength and mercy. Then he ordered them to take up their weapons, form their ranks, and be quick about it all. This done, he led his soldiers, marching silently, fighting back the uneasiness in the stomach and the trembling in the hand, through the frosted woods that cluttered the base of Ashdown. After a short march, they spilled out of the woods and onto the rising slope of the battleground, into the full view of the Viking throng.

Upon seeing the arrival of the men of Wessex, the Vikings erupted into a barrage of derisive howls and jeers. The Viking taunt was a studied and oft-practiced literary genre among the Danish warriors. The subject matter of this mockery moved from general observations about the cowardice of the opponent and how his corpse would soon be fed to birds, to more personal speculations about the various womenfolk waiting behind in the Wessex villages, and usually culminated in the accusation that the men of Wessex actually lacked any natural affections for women in the first place. Though it may have been easy for Alfred to ignore the content of the Danish insults, what could not be ignored was that the Viking warriors, who swarmed the crest of the hill above, were utterly unafraid of the battle to come. In fact, they hungered for it with a bemusing confidence.

But far more dismaying to Alfred than the taunting force on the hillside ahead was the absence on either flank of his brother and the second half of the Wessex army. The plan had been for both Alfred and Æthelred to immediately muster their forces and march to face the Danes. But Æthelred was nowhere in sight. Alfred would later learn that after the two had made their battle plans and separated, Æthelred had returned to his tent and summoned his priest in order that he might hear mass before facing the morning's combat. The king was late for battle because, as the historian would later explain, he was lingering long in his prayers.

Whether Æthelred had expected Alfred to take longer to muster his troops or whether he had been overwhelmed by the moment, is unrecorded. It would be understandable if Æthelred had felt a little more fear than Alfred at the prospect of charging into this particular battle. Considering the fates of the previous Anglo-Saxon kings who had lost to the invading Northmen, there was a uniquely gory risk that the king took in picking up his sword for this fight.

The Wessex army appeared to the Vikings to be much smaller than expected and were also transparently bewildered and unprepared for combat. The Viking commanders saw a welcome opportunity and commanded their men to attack. Alfred stood with only half of the Wessex army, looking confusedly about him, unsure whether he should wait for his brother to appear or quickly withdraw his men.

Next the confusion turned to desperation when he saw the Viking men above, stretched out in battle array and beginning to advance. Unprepared and halved in strength, how could his men face the descending swarm?

But it was clear that withdrawing his men was no longer an option. If he pulled his men from the battlefield, the Vikings would hotly pursue. Then the men of Wessex would be chased through the forests like hunted rabbits and their corpses strewn all along the Berkshire Downs. Alfred had run from the Viking army only four days before. As terrifying as the battle line before him may have been, he knew that he preferred to face the crashing wave of Vikings head-on, rather than to be hunted and cut down from behind.

Alfred gave the command to form the shieldwall.

Even as early as the time of Alfred, the shieldwall was already considered an ancient tactic, hearkening all the way back to the ancient Greek hoplites of the seventh century BC. It consisted simply of a line of men standing shoulder to shoulder with their shields overlapping one another, forming a continuous wall of protection. This line of shields was supported by a depth of approximately ten ranks of additional soldiers positioned behind the front line, leaning into the front rank to allow them to hold their ground and stay locked together (not unlike a rugby scrum). This tight formation had the potential to be virtually impenetrable, provided that the courage and endurance of the soldiers held. Having formed the shieldwall, the Wessex army was prepared to face the oncoming crush of the Viking horde. Alfred joined the shieldwall, standing shoulder to shoulder with his men. The notion of being led into battle by a man who wasn't willing to personally lead the charge would have been unthinkable to the men of Wessex.

As the two armies closed on each other, the various taunts and jeers of the Viking throng began to coalesce into a steady guttural rumble that rolled down the hillside. The deep rumble grew ever louder until that moment—after a seemingly interminable approach—when the first spear tip drove hard into the defiant shieldwall and the valley shook with the crack of the collision. Every nervous stomach, every quivering hand, every dry tongue, all foreboding fears and presentiments, were instantly transformed into resolution and determination; and the shieldwall erupted with a deafening war cry.

Much to the surprise of the Viking army, the Wessex shieldwall not only held after the first impact, but it began to push the Viking force backward almost immediately after that initial impact. The sensation for Alfred's men was probably similar to the feeling a boy has in his first athletic competition, when he suddenly realizes he is equal to his opponent who had seemed so invincible when considered from a distance. Emboldened by the initial success of the shieldwall, the Anglo-Saxons began to slash and hack their way forward, pushing hard against the Viking host, driving them back up the hillside.

Alfred's biographer later emphasized the rightness of the cause of the Wessex soldiers, a confidence that their fight was just and that God was on their side. The intensity of the fight, the thrill of the early success, the confidence of divine favor, all worked powerfully on Alfred, awakening a savage fury in him. His men later described him as a wild boar on the battlefield, a bloody beast, rampaging through the Viking lines in a ruthless rage. On and on the combat continued, swirling around a lone thorn tree. Many years after the battle was over, veterans would come and point with pride to that thorn tree, which marked the very spot on the hillside where they had stood with Alfred and fought in the battle of Ashdown.

The surprising strength with which the Wessex shieldwall resisted the initial Viking charge may have sent a momentary disappointment through the Danish host. They quickly converted their hope for an easy victory into an indefatigable determination to bathe the slopes of Ashdown in Wessex blood. Soon the ground gained by Saxon troops was being slowly granted back again to the Viking horde, passing the lonely thorn tree once more.

A well-formed shieldwall was virtually impenetrable, so long as the wall held together. If a gap could be cut into the wall, then the enemy would pour through the line and attack from behind, where the wall was vulnerable. Once a hole was cut into the shieldwall, even if for just a moment, the sudden attack of enemy soldiers from behind made it impossible to keep the formation together; the shieldwall would be abandoned quickly, and general chaos would ensue. Thus, most methods for assaulting the wall focused on ripping open the wall, hoping to capitalize on the bedlam that inevitably followed.

An attack would come as a sudden hard push, a human battering ram, where one shieldwall tried to outmuscle the other. In this type of engagement, the primary weapon was the spear. Instead of being thrown, the spear was kept in hand and thrust over and in between the shields. The spear's length made it possible to wield it effectively against the enemy while standing several ranks back from the front line of the shieldwall. A Norse manual would later insist that a spear was worth two swords when fighting against a shieldwall.

Swords and axes were more difficult to wield in such close quarters and tended to be reserved for hand-to-hand combat in the many smaller skirmishes that followed once the shieldwall had broken. It was possible, however, to use the bottom of the axe head to hook an opposing shield and pull it away to leave its owner vulnerable to a spear thrust. Additionally, many soldiers carried a sax, a much shorter sword with a blade of one to two feet. A sax could be much more easily wielded inside the tight confines of the shieldwall. Swords and axes may have also been useful for attacking the unprotected legs of the enemy, but the awkwardness of swinging such bulky weapons within the confines of the shieldwall, however, made the spear the weapon of choice.

Though the Wessex shieldwall continued to hold, the casualties inflicted by the Viking attack began to mount. The Danish spearmen constantly wormed their deadly spears through the network of shields, searching for the tender flesh of the Wessex front rank.

Each time the spear was driven home—sometimes with a deadly precision to the neck or abdomen, but more often catching some Saxon in a less vital area like the thigh or an unprotected shoulder—the wall was weakened by one. These wounds may not have been immediately fatal, but the pain and blood loss removed the soldier from the fight.[2]

The Wessex line now required endurance and discipline to hold together throughout this cruel battle of bloody attrition. As each warrior fell, his place had to be filled quickly and willingly by the man standing immediately behind him. A moment's hesitation, a moment of considering what price might be paid for filling that gap, and a hole was left open for a horde of Vikings to pour through the shieldwall, ending the battle. And once a man took a position in the front rank, there could be no turning back. He was woven into a wall of shields that utterly depended on his constant struggle to hold the line together.

When a shieldwall did fail, it was almost inevitably not from the power of the attacking army, but from cowardice in the ranks of the shieldwall. If a man ripped himself from the wall and turned to run, it would trigger a chain reaction in all those around him, and the entire wall would dissolve in seconds. One man running from fear

[2] In an age when the importance of a thorough cleaning of the wound was not adequately understood, there was a high likelihood that many of the cuts and gashes would become septic. Anglo-Saxon poetry often referred to the blades and spear points of their enemies as "poisonous," and when taking into account the likelihood of a deadly infection following a more superficial wound, there was good reason to have thought so. Many of these stab wounds would become unnecessarily lethal a few days following the combat.

was far more damaging to the integrity of the wall than twenty men falling from stab wounds.

The movements of the shieldwall were not coordinated from afar. Generals could not sit at a safe distance from the conflict sending messengers into the fray with orders for troop movements and changes of tactics. After the command to form the shieldwall had been given, the only leadership the soldiers required was the leadership of example. The commander joined his men, standing shoulder to shoulder with them throughout the gruesome conflict. While he stood and fought, they stood and fought. If he fell, a spirit of hopelessness would smother the spirit in his men, and the battle would immediately turn against them. If he fled, there was absolutely no reason for the men to stay and fight, so the battlefield would empty in moments. Alfred, though completely new to this responsibility, held his place and fought on, the wild boar rampaging across the slopes of Ashdown.

And then without warning, the inexorable Viking assault suddenly dissolved. In one moment, the fierce and relentless barrage of Danish warriors vanished as if it had been a mirage. All that was left was a view of the backside of a panic-stricken mob fleeing for its life. It took several moments for Alfred and his men to recover from their amazement and to realize what had happened. Suddenly, it became clear.

King Æthelred had finished his prayers.

The Viking commanders had not realized that the Wessex troops they had engaged represented only half of the army they would be facing that day. Thus, when they had stood on the summit of Ashdown to watch Alfred lead his meager force onto the slope below and form his men into a shieldwall, they confidently advanced the entirety of their army on that one small troop. Though they may have been surprised by the strength of the Wessex shieldwall during their initial assault, they were confident that their vastly superior numbers would enable them to win.

With their sudden appearance, King Æthelred and his men not only removed the Viking advantage of outnumbering the men of Wessex but also were perfectly poised to attack the unprotected flank of the Viking shieldwall. The Vikings were utterly defenseless as the second half of the Wessex army charged onto the battlefield and drove straight for the vulnerable flank of the Viking line.

The appearance, however, of Æthelred and his men did not signal an abrupt end of combat; rather, it meant a major transition in the nature of the fighting as the Vikings grew more and more desperate. The Danish shieldwall crumpled in seconds as astonishment at the sudden appearance of another Saxon army turned to raw fear. The Viking force, which had moved as one only moments before, now dissolved into a thousand bands of individual warriors no longer fighting to drive the Saxons from the battlefield but now merely trying to find a way to free themselves from the clutches of Wessex. Those who were able to hack their way free from the melee sprinted for the safety of the woods, but those who found themselves surrounded by the Saxon forces were forced to fight on in smaller, more chaotic, skirmishes. No longer encumbered by the shieldwall, the hand-to-hand combat turned to a more one-on-one style of fighting where each combatant relied solely on his own quickness of sword or axe and general cunning.

The gruesome fighting continued for several hours until the entire Viking host had either fallen or fled and the men of Wessex once again dominated Ashdown. Those Vikings who fled were chased throughout that evening and into the next day, when they were finally able to find refuge behind the fortifications of Viking-held Reading. Those who fell in battle, numbering well into the thousands, became plunder for the victorious Anglo-Saxons.

Possession of the battlefield meant much more than clear military triumph. It also meant the right to plunder the dead. Because the Viking force traveled with much of its wealth on its back, the booty that could be collected from the bodies of the fallen was substantial. As the dead were searched for coins, jewelry, and other portable wealth, the bodies of a number of Viking chieftains were discovered. Among the dead were the Viking king, Bagsecg, as well as five Viking earls—Earl Sidroc the Elder, Earl Sidroc the Younger, Earl Osbern, Earl Fræna, and Earl Harold.

Once the battle was truly over, Æthelred and Alfred began to accept their victory. The enemy had been routed, leaving the corpses of thousands littering what the Anglo-Saxon tongue would refer to as "the place of slaughter." The Viking leadership was well represented among the dead, and what was left of the raiding army had limped back to Reading. For that brief moment, it seemed as if the Creator had smiled upon them, and their fortunes could have been no better.

But fortunes fade quickly. King Æthelred and his brother Alfred soon discovered that, despite the good name they had won on the slopes of Ashdown and the plunder the triumphant men of Wessex had carted off, the victory had cost the Saxon forces a price just as high as the price paid by the raiding army of Vikings. From the initial contact between the Viking foraging party and the small army led by Æthelwulf, the Berkshire ealdorman, to the great victory at Ashdown, the number of the Wessex slain throughout this campaign was equal to the significant casualties suffered by the Viking armies.

The loss of life affected the Saxons differently than it did the Vikings, however. The Viking raiding army was filled with professional soldiers, men whose absence from home left no significant gap in the local economy. But the men of Wessex who had fallen in battle were not professional soldiers. They were farmers and craftsmen. When they failed to return from battle, crops failed and villages went hungry. Even those who returned from the battles victorious and unscathed still suffered loss. Their fields had been left untended too long. The work had piled up. Men who lived productive lives growing food for others and caring for the various needs of their villages could not afford to spend months of time wandering the countryside of Wessex, searching out the Danish bandits.

The men of the raiding armies lived off theft and not labor. Their parasitic diet of pillage and plunder made it impossible to stay behind the walls of Reading for any period of time. Thus the livelihood of Wessex depended on its troops returning home to work, while the livelihood of the raiding army depended on their continued ravaging of the countryside.

In the days immediately following their tremendous victory, Æthelred and Alfred found it impossible to maintain an army large enough to follow up their hard-fought victory with an assault on the Viking stronghold in Reading. Having driven the Danes back to their makeshift fortress, one last decisive attack on the Viking camp would rid Wessex entirely of the raiding army, but the war-weary and wounded men of Wessex felt they had been absent from their home villages for far too long. During the next few days, an endless parade of men filed out of the Wessex camp, returning to the countless villages of the countryside.

Soon Æthelred and Alfred were left with only a skeleton of an army, hardly the mighty force they had led to victory at Ashdown. Still, they moved their camp close to the Viking fortress at Reading and looked for opportunities to harass the Danes as they recovered from their wounds. For months, this meant primarily looking to intercept the smaller Viking scavenging parties as they scoured the countryside in search of supplies. Alfred spent the bulk of his time during these months leading smaller bands of Wessex soldiers on horseback, hunting for Danish plunderers in the environs surrounding Reading.

Although the few brief hours of combat at the battle of Ashdown had taught him much about war, the following months offered him his first prolonged study of the people who were to become his lifelong nemeses. Day after day, he learned to transfer the skill of tracking and hunting the wild beasts of England's woods, which he had honed throughout his youth, to the skill of tracking and hunting his enemy. He studied their customs and habits, what tactics were effective, and how to predict their movements. And he also studied the men whom Æthelred had entrusted to him—what motivated them, how to use their strengths most effectively, and what their greatest weaknesses were.

Two things became clear during the course of Alfred's studies. First, there was nothing superhuman about the Viking warrior. Alfred had seen clearly that an Anglo-Saxon warrior was more than capable of holding his own against a Viking combatant in an equal fight. Alfred had drawn Viking blood, and he knew he could kill them. But the second thing that became more and more apparent as the frigid winter months dragged on was that the inability of Wessex to keep a sizable force armed and prepared to fight was crippling their chances of overcoming the Viking invaders.

This second lesson was driven home only two weeks after the battle of Ashdown. The Viking army ventured out once more in full force and began marching directly toward Winchester, the capital of Wessex. It is unlikely the Viking army really intended to strike at Winchester at this point, but the boldness of this move demanded that the severely weakened army of Wessex respond. Æthelred and Alfred led their men to intercept the advancing Vikings at Basing, nineteen miles south of Reading. Once more the two shieldwalls clashed. But this time the thinness of the Wessex wall would receive no miraculous reinforcements halfway through the battle. Despite a valiant effort to hold off the Viking advance, the shieldwall soon gave way, and the Saxons were forced to retreat in humiliation, conceding the place of slaughter to the raiding army.

The defeat at Basing was a bitter disappointment and an ill portent of things to come. However, it was not an entirely devastating loss. The Viking troops were not able to pursue the Saxon troops and inflict the same kind of punishment on the Wessex soldiers as the Northmen had received at Ashdown. The Viking approach toward Winchester was halted at Basing, so the battle at Basing was not an all-out loss. But Basing became just the first in a series of defeats that slowly pushed the Saxon forces backward as the Viking grip on the throat of Wessex tightened each week.

Alfred continued to lead a small host of men to harass and harry the occasional Viking foraging parties, but he found it impossible to muster a force large enough to assault the fortifications at Reading and drive the Vikings completely off Wessex soil. Even worse, as the winter months came to an end and the spring sun climbed higher in the sky, the possibility grew that any day another wave of Danish troops might cross the channel to join the raiding army and try their luck at plundering Wessex.

At this point, the perilous position of the nation of Wessex became more and more evident to Æthelred and Alfred. The fall of Northumbria and Essex, and the complete capitulation of Mercia, left Wessex standing defiantly alone against the Viking invaders. The precariousness of their position impressed upon the two brothers the constant need for an experienced and respected leader, whom all of Wessex could follow with complete loyalty. There was a real need to formalize on paper what might have already been assumed between the two brothers about the succession of the crown. Uncertainty on this point threatened to bring calamitous civil unrest if the king of Wessex should have an untimely death.

With this concern in mind, a *witan*, a meeting of the wise men of Wessex, was summoned to Swinbeorg to discuss the succession of the crown. The *witan* provided the opportunity to receive the wisdom of the elders of the nation, without which no successful king of Wessex could rule. Here it was decided that, between Æthelred and Alfred, the brother to survive the longest would claim the throne for himself and his sons. Great care was taken to ensure provision for the sons of the brother who perished first. When their father, Æthelwulf, had died, he had divided a collection of private estates among each of his five sons.

With Solomonic insight, it was decided before the *witan* that the brother to ultimately inherit the crown would ensure that the children of the deceased received the share of these estates that had been passed on to their father, as well as the share of the estates received by the still living, and then ruling, son. Essentially the brothers agreed that in exchange for the crown the surviving brother would forfeit a portion of his own inheritance to his nephews.

Two months after Basing, a well-rested Viking army moved out once more in full force to challenge whatever troops Æthelred and Alfred were able to assemble. Despite the importance of spring work on the Saxon farms, a significant force gathered to Æthelred when the call to arms was given. Overtaking the Danes at Merton, the Saxons attempted to repeat their earlier tactic of splitting their men into two units, one commanded by Æthelred and the other by Alfred. Once more, the Saxon shieldwall stood stouthearted and ready for the battle rush. Once more, they drove their ashen spears hard into the enemy line with a deafening crack and a roar of righteous wrath.

Again the two foes stood within a few feet of one another, stabbing and slashing at every piece of flesh or bone left unprotected or uncovered in the shieldwall. With blow after earthshaking blow, the two armies worked at one another like blacksmiths, hammering away defiantly at one another's iron will. And once more, after hours of deadly diligence, the Viking line began to crumble. Just as before, after the Viking line began to break, the entire Danish horde sprinted from the battlefield, leaving the weary Saxons elated in their exhaustion.

But unlike before, the Viking retreat was only temporary. The Saxon forces, failing to press the retreat hard and drive the running soldiers into the sort of frenzied panic they had achieved at Ashdown, had thought their victory was sealed and relaxed their pursuit. The flood of Danes streaming from the battlefield began to slow and form again into another shieldwall, and the retreat turned into a regrouping. Soon the jubilation of the temporarily triumphant Saxons dissolved, and they began frantically reforming their shield-wall to hold off another swelling attack. Again the Viking crush rushed over the Saxon shieldwall, and, like the successive waves of an incoming tide, this second breaker came harder and stronger than before. The shield-wall shivered and splintered, and the men of Wessex lost hope in one chaotic instant.

Æthelred and Alfred lost all control of their men as the entire Wessex army fled madly, leaving the Viking host the proud masters of the place of slaughter. In the panicked retreat, countless Saxons were cut down. By the time the field had cleared, the ground was littered with the dead, both Viking and Saxon. Most tragically for the people of Wessex, the good bishop of Sherborne, Bishop Heahmund, was among the dead on the field of the slain.[3] But even

[3] Anglo-Saxon Britain had, of course, a very different set of expectations for their clergy than that of the modern church. Priests and bishops were expected to be leaders of men, and this obligation didn't vanish during times of war. Thus Anglo-Saxon armies were often commanded by members of the clergy who, like Heahmund, fought and died along with the men of their parishes.

more seriously, when Alfred was finally able to find his brother in the panicked retreat, he discovered that Æthelred had been gravely wounded.

During the next several weeks, Æthelred's condition grew worse and worse. Weakened from the initial loss of blood, the king's body now slowly began to succumb to the infections that swelled his gory wounds. The leeching of the court healers, though likely well-intentioned, did little to reverse his gradual decline into a tormented and feverish delirium. As the fallen king's cuts turned septic, the festering wounds reopened again and again, spilling blood and puss, and giving off a suffocating stench. Though those who cared for him gave themselves to hopeful prayer for his recovery, the certain death of the king loomed over the court of Wessex.

Under the shadow of this morbid expectation, Alfred greeted the Easter of 871. The grim mood of the Wessex court could have easily made celebrating a festival such as Easter nearly impossible, but there was a certain resonance between Alfred's personal story and the gospel narrative declared in the Easter liturgy. Easter promised a hope beyond death. In fact, Easter promised a hope that came as a direct result of death. Easter told the story of one man's fatal sacrifice, a sacrifice that conquered death by first seeming to give in to death. At Easter, Alfred was reminded of a resurrection that undid all the suffering of death.

Taking this message to heart might have changed how Alfred interpreted the state of Wessex. Perhaps even in this time of terrible darkness, even as all of Wessex was slowly engulfed by an ever-advancing godless foe, even as the king of Wessex writhed in a fatal agony, perhaps God was about to bring about a resurrecting deliverance in their midst.

If Alfred thought this, he could not have been more wrong. Immediately after Easter, King Æthelred died. After mourning the death of his brother, Alfred received the crown of Wessex, and the burden of defending her fell squarely on his shoulders. Shortly after this, he received news that a fresh fleet of Viking ships had just arrived at Reading to join Halfdan. Sailing up the Thames, this fleet brought thousands of new Viking men intent on quick plunder, led by three new Viking kings—Guthrum, Oscetel, and Anwend. Word had spread of the easy wealth to be gained from looting the English countryside. Vikings who had been scattered all along the rivers of the European continent now focused their attentions on the island of Britain. The easily gotten gold drew them from thousands of miles away—a ninth-century gold rush.

CHAPTER 4

Danegeld

It is always a temptation to an armed and agile nation,
To call upon a neighbour and to say:
"We invaded you last night—we are quite
    prepared to fight,
Unless you pay us cash to go away."

And that is called asking for Dane-geld,
And the people who ask it explain
That you've only to pay 'em the Dane-geld
And then you'll get rid of the Dane!

It is always a temptation to a rich and lazy nation,
To puff and look important and to say:
"Though we know we should defeat you, we have
    not the time to meet you.
We will therefore pay you cash to go away."

And that is called paying the Dane-geld;
But we've proved it again and again,
That if once you have paid him the Dane-geld
You never get rid of the Dane.

It is wrong to put temptation in the path of any
    nation,

For fear they should succumb and go astray,
So when you are requested to pay up or be
    molested,
You will find it better policy to say:

"We never pay any-one Dane-geld,
No matter how trifling the cost,
For the end of that game is oppression and shame,
And the nation that plays it is lost!"

—RUDYARD KIPLING, "DANE-GELD"

I n AD 871, Alfred received a heavy crown,
weighted with the responsibility of protecting
a kingdom on the brink of conquest, the last
Anglo-Saxon nation to remain standing against the
Viking invasion. Throughout that spring, the raiding army pushed deeper and deeper into the heart of
Wessex. On the very day Alfred attended Æthelred's
funeral at Wimbourne Minster (a church later to be
destroyed by raiding Danes), Wessex forces con-
fronted a Viking host who had poured out of Reading
to rampage and plunder throughout the northeastern
regions of the nation. The Wessex resistance had

grown weaker, however, and more and more of these Viking pillaging forays went unchecked.

Finally, one month after Æthelred's death, Alfred led the Wessex army out in a desperate attempt at drawing the Danes into a decisive battle, hoping to halt the Viking advance. Alfred's forces caught the Viking army at Wilton, less than thirty miles east of Winchester. The proximity of this battle to Alfred's capital city was clear proof that the Viking conquest of Wessex was making very steady progress, venturing deeper and deeper into the heart of the young ruler's kingdom.

The Wessex army was significantly depleted by the carnage of this war. Alfred's biographer recorded that at this point, in addition to countless smaller skirmishes, the armies of Wessex had fought eight separate battles against the Vikings and had been virtually annihilated. Englefield, Reading, Ashdown, Basing, Merton, and several other unnamed battles had taken a serious toll on the Wessex shieldwall. Conversely, the Viking army was now swollen with fresh recruits, newly arrived from the European continent and hungry for plunder.

But it wasn't just the casualties of war that had so weakened the shieldwalls of Wessex. The awkwardness of the Anglo-Saxon military structure was an important factor in the depletion of forces. Though Alfred had his own contingent of professional warriors attached to his court, their number was small, less than a hundred men, and hardly constituted an army. Whenever the king of Wessex needed to gather an army to fend off an enemy invasion, it was necessary that he assemble the *fyrd*, a voluntary ad hoc militia.

The numerous landowning noblemen of Wessex, the ealdormen who commanded the loyalty of the local farmers and craftsmen of the individual shires, held the fyrd together. These ealdormen ruled the shires on the king's behalf, enforcing the rule of law, ensuring that taxes were gathered, and preparing the shires to defend themselves in case of attack. Each ealdorman had the ability to summon a fyrd from his shire, a force numbering up to several thousand men. Then when a national emergency arose, the king could call his ealdormen, along with their shire fyrds, creating one large national fyrd, numbering as many as ten thousand men. The fyrd system totally depended on the corresponding obligations of a man to his lord and the lord back to his subjects. These simple instincts, the faithfulness to a master and the love for a people, forged a strong and compelling bond that time and again held the warriors of Wessex together in the clash of the shieldwalls.

But there was a clumsiness and inefficiency to this system as well. First, this was not a standing army. This was a force that had to be summoned for each individual action, a process that could take weeks to complete. Armies that moved and struck swiftly, like the Viking raiding armies, had way too much time to advance untouched. Second, because the fyrd was composed of a loose combination of smaller shire fyrds, the national fyrd had very geographically divided loyalties. For instance, when the national fyrd was involved in a retreating campaign, as Alfred was at this point, the various shire fyrds often dropped out of the army as their shire was conquered.

These men were prompted to drop out of the war not because of cowardice but because of a need to return to protect their families who now lived behind the lines of an advancing enemy. So once the Wessex fyrd had lost the battle at Merton, the men of Berkshire and Hampshire returned to their homes to protect their families from the raping and plundering Viking conquerors while the rest of the Wessex army moved on to the next battle at Wilton. No matter how noble this defection may have been, it continually depleted the Wessex battle lines.

The disparity between these two forces became all too clear once the two shieldwalls lined up to face one another on the battlefield of Wilton. The haggard Wessex line was dwarfed by the enormous Viking troop. Whatever misgivings Alfred may have had about the number of Wessex warriors, however, once the shieldwall was formed, there was no choice but to move resolutely into battle. Although now an experienced veteran of several gruesome battles with this particular enemy, this was the first time Alfred would lead the men of Wessex into battle as their king. If he wanted to continue to command his men's respect and loyalty, it was important that he conduct himself throughout the battle courageously and decisively.

Surprisingly, the initial clash again favored the men of Wessex. The shieldwall held against the massive Viking onslaught, and the men of Wessex unleashed a torrent of punishing blows on the front rank of the Viking swarm. Whether it was an innate quality in the Wessex blood or perhaps a common quality that arises in men who defend their homeland, the soldiers of Wessex regularly managed to hold their ground despite being significantly outnumbered. The Viking forces—fighting only for the opportunity to plunder their opponents—were less driven. Lacking the frenzied desperation that drove their opponent, the Viking forces were often easily repulsed. And so the battle of Wilton raged throughout the day. The Danish forces learned that what the Saxon shieldwall lacked in numbers was more than compensated by grim resolve.

Soon the Viking troop grew weary of the attack, and their shieldwall began to falter and crumble. Once their protective formation had failed, there was no choice for the Danes but to run from the field, leaving Alfred standing bewilderingly triumphant with his exhausted men on the battlefield.

However, the warriors of Wessex had failed to learn an important lesson from their experience at the battle of Merton. Just as at Merton, the Saxons had driven the Viking force from the battlefield without pressing the retreat, and once more the men of Wessex stood reveling in their victory and enjoying a seemingly well-earned rest instead of pursuing the enemy. The retreating Viking horde soon sensed this tactical blunder, and the Viking flight quickly transformed into a regrouping for the next attack. A moment later, as the Danish line came rumbling forward once more, the thrill of victory converted instantly into a nauseating dread as the men of the Wessex line attempted to reform. However, the spirit had been knocked out of Alfred's army, and the feeble attempt at a second shieldwall was easily overwhelmed. Soon it was the men of Wessex who were running from the battlefield, leaving the place of slaughter and the plunder ripe for the victorious raiding army.

Of the many battles now fought between Wessex and the raiding army, Wessex had won only the smaller conflict at Englefield and the great battle of Ashdown. In every other engagement, the victory had ultimately gone to the Danish marauders, whose advance seemed inexorable and certain. It was difficult at this time for Alfred to imagine how his people could continue resisting these relentless invaders. Despite how grim things may have seemed for the people of Wessex, it likely would have been surprising to them to discover that the Viking kings were growing frustrated and impatient with their own progress. The resistance of all the other Saxon kingdoms had crumbled quickly after one decisive battle. No Saxon kingdom had put up anywhere near the resistance that Wessex had. Even when Wessex lost a battle, it did so at such a great cost to the Viking numbers that, in the end, the Viking victory was negligible.

The Danes had grown anxious to find a more profitable prey, a people who would surrender their wealth more eagerly. And so, shortly after the battle of Wilton, the Vikings settled on a deal with Alfred to end their occupation of Wessex. The accounts of this arrangement give no details and say only that Alfred made peace with the Vikings on the condition that they would move on. It is fairly certain, however, that "made peace" is a nicer way of saying that Alfred paid the Vikings an enormous sum of money in exchange for their withdrawal. This payment was known commonly as the *danegeld*, a ransom paid for peace. It may seem strange to think that at the very moment when the Viking army was finally positioned to crush the Wessex resistance, they were suddenly willing to abandon their prospects of conquest and settle for a quick cash payment after pursuing a protracted, bloody, and unprofitable campaign in Wessex for so long. For more than a century, however, the raiding armies of Northmen had cultivated a habit of searching out the path of least resistance to plunder. They had begun with the unguarded riches of monasteries and then moved on to the wealth easily extracted from weak kings and small nations on the brink of collapse. The campaign in Wessex had been too costly for the Danes, who preferred much more easily gotten spoils.

The Viking army happily received the offer of danegeld, promptly abandoned their fortress at Reading, and withdrew to Mercian London, weighed down with the wealth of Wessex as they traveled.

The wisdom of paying the danegeld has been much debated throughout the years, spurred on by Kipling's summary of the lesson to be learned from this chapter of history—"if once you pay him the Dane-geld, you never get rid of the Dane." Scholars tend to dismiss Kipling's wisdom as naïvely idealistic and unacquainted with the real-world complications of kingship. Kipling's policy may seem ever so noble and heroic, but many would suggest that sometimes survival requires a number of very ignoble and unheroic choices. Many would argue that Alfred's payment of the danegeld was the most prudent course of action that realistically could have been pursued.

No matter how overly idealistic Kipling's foreign policy may have been, it can't be denied there was a good deal of truth to the poet's conclusion. Paying the danegeld never buys more than short-term peace. The payment reveals a weakness, a willingness to give up wealth without a fight. And, like the scent of blood to sharks, this message could do nothing other than attract future Viking attacks.

A century later, Alfred's great, great grandson, Æthelred II, would pursue a disastrous policy of regularly paying the danegeld, which resulted in a series of successive Danish invasions, each of which was rewarded by an even larger payment of the danegeld. Eventually the Danes gained control of all of England, and King Æthelred II was exiled. This was the course Alfred himself had begun to take.

Not only did Alfred's decision guarantee future Danish campaigns into Wessex, but it also required Alfred to raise an enormous amount of money for the danegeld payment, an amount he was not capable of personally producing from his royal holdings. This meant that Alfred must exact from his people a sudden, enormous, and unreasonable tax, a tax that fell primarily on the churches, the largest haven of wealth in the ninth century. In the years to come, a number of Wessex churches would find it hard to forgive Alfred for the financial burden that was put onto them in the summer of 871.

Alfred's decision to pay the danegeld could not have come at a better time for the Viking commander, Halfdan. Not only had Halfdan's army grown terribly weary of the heavy losses brought on by the Wessex campaign, but also the Viking grip on the other Anglo-Saxon territories had begun to fail during the prolonged invasion of Wessex. In the early winter months of 872, the Danes returned to London, where they again successfully demanded danegeld from the Mercian king, Burgred, Alfred's brother-in-law. Accepting the danegeld obligated the Vikings to leave the Mercian kingdom, and Halfdan soon had his men on the move once more. The departure from London, however, had less to do with honoring an agreement with King Burgred and more to do with reasserting Viking control over the Anglo-Saxons in general. While wintering in London, Halfdan received word that the Northumbrians had taken advantage of the long Viking absence and had cast out the puppet king and bishop whom the Danes had installed in York.

In response to this rebellion, Halfdan led his forces from London north to Torksey, a town that lay inside the borders of Mercia but was ideally located for forays into Northumbria. At Torksey, a canal connected the Trent to the river Witham, giving the Danish army passageways deep into Northumbria, Mercia, and East Anglia. The site was ideal for reminding these conquered nations of the Viking supremacy.

Torksey lay within the borders of Mercia, meaning the Viking army had not left King Burgred's borders, despite having taken his danegeld. This alarmed the weak Mercian king, who soon began to wonder if the Vikings planned to betray their implicit agreement that he was allowed to rule Mercia if he would regularly bow and scrape before the Danish rulers. Burgred attempted to appease the Viking overlords by welcoming into his court the puppet king and bishop whom the Northumbrians had ousted. Then, to make his subservience doubly clear, Burgred paid Halfdan the danegeld one more time.

Not surprisingly, Burgred's attempts at conciliation only hastened the end of his reign. Rather than gratefully receiving Burgred's desperate offers of friendship and peace, the Danes sensed profound weakness in the Mercian king, a weakness that begged to be exploited. Immediately after accepting the second offering of danegeld, Halfdan sent a small force sailing up the Trent to Repton, where they constructed a small earthen fortress along the riverbank. Though the force was not large enough to launch a viable assault on Burgred in Nottingham, the move still spooked the jittery Mercian king. Burgred immediately abandoned Nottingham and fled England along with his wife Ælswith, Alfred's sister.

The Mercian king and queen left their thrones to become pilgrims of the holy city of Rome. Soon their names were entered into the book of guests recorded by the monks of Brescia, the same book that had recorded Alfred's pilgrimage as a young boy. Burgred and Ælswith took up residence in the Saxon quarter of Rome, where Alfred and his father had lived during their visit. Burgred was later buried in the Church of Saint Maria in the *Schola Saxonum*, which Alfred's father had renovated during his visit.

The Mercian throne was then filled by a Danish appointment—Ceolwulf, a puppet king—much like the king the Danes had previously left in charge of Northumbria. Ceolwulf would later be remembered as a foolish and worthless stooge of his Danish masters. At this point, the Viking army split up. Halfdan led a force to the north to crush the Northumbrian rebellion, and Guthrum led another army to Cambridge in East Anglia, from where he would control East Anglia and Mercia.

For Alfred, the Northumbrian rebellion and the collapse of Mercia may have seemed to provide a welcome respite in that it demanded the Danish forces to devote their attention elsewhere for several years. However, this interlude allowed the Vikings to more firmly establish their grip on the rest of Britain, and it put them in a much more powerful position from which to launch their next assault on Wessex. Had Alfred used these years well and addressed the real weaknesses of the Wessex defenses, the Viking kings may have regretted giving him several years of peace. Even though Alfred was keenly aware of where the Wessex army had fallen short, he still lacked either the insight or the means to address these shortcomings.

During these few years, the Wessex king heard regular reports about the conquests by the Danish armies throughout Britain. All the while, he was at a loss as to how he would be able to withstand the next invasion.

Sensing that a renewed Viking attack on his nation was imminent, Alfred ensured that the borders of Wessex were carefully watched. This meant a vigilant watch over all the possible avenues of approach, including the vulnerable southern coastline. With this in mind, he worked hard at developing a small naval force that might be able to fend off some of the smaller Viking attacks.

In the year 875, Alfred received word of a Viking fleet approaching the shores of Wessex. To Alfred's relief, there were only seven ships in this small raiding army. Clearly the goal of this fleet was plunder and not conquest. Nevertheless, Alfred personally led the ships of Wessex to intercept the Viking boats. In this brief engagement, one Viking ship was captured, and the other six were put to flight. The victory was small, but sweet. The following year, a much more formidable attack was launched against Wessex. This time the intention was not merely looting and plundering but all-out conquest.

In the year 876, the Viking king, Guthrum, leader of the Danish forces occupying East Anglia, led his army out of Cambridge under the cover of darkness and began a hasty march toward Wessex. Combining the secrecy of swift nighttime marches with a route carefully chosen to minimize any encounters with the forces of Wessex, Guthrum was able to lead his Danish army, virtually unnoticed, through the heart of Wessex all the way to the southern coast. Whatever improvements Alfred had made to Wessex's ability to respond to a raiding army, they were proved utterly futile by this one march. By the time Alfred received word of the Danish intrusion and began to muster his army in response, Guthrum had already seized the strategically located town of Wareham and begun to fortify his position against Saxon attacks.

Once again, the Vikings had chosen an ideally located position for their base of operations. Wareham was bounded on the north by the river Tarrant and on the south by the river Frome. The two rivers merged just past the city, on the eastern side, and then dumped into Poole Bay. These waterways provided highly effective defenses on three of the city's four sides and offered passage to Viking longboats, the preferred means of travel for the Danish raiders striking deep into the heart of Wessex and of providing reinforcement from the sea. The western side of the city was defended by one long earthen rampart. Wareham was the site of an ancient Anglo-Saxon convent, which meant it offered the sort of undefended ecclesiastical wealth the Vikings so appreciated, as well as a number of highly productive farms. Between the two rivers and Wareham's earthen fortifications, the Vikings had access to around one hundred acres of land. Guthrum had chosen his beachhead well.

Alfred arrived with the army of Wessex shortly after Guthrum's men had settled into their new fortress. The fact that the Vikings had been able to march straight through the heart of Wessex, reaching all the way to the southern coast, and then capture and fortify a village *before* the Wessex fyrd was able to form was clear proof of how fatally flawed the fyrd system had become. By the time Alfred's men arrived, Guthrum had dug in and was more than prepared to resist any assault on the well-defended town of Wareham.

Remembering the disastrous attack that Æthelred and Alfred had launched against the Viking fortifications at Reading, Alfred was hesitant to begin another assault on the rampart of Wareham. He chose instead to lay siege to Wareham, cutting off the Danes' ability to send out foraging parties and hoping to starve the Vikings out of their new lair. But it soon became apparent that Guthrum was far too well prepared. The Vikings were amply supplied and, much like the earlier episode at Nottingham, were likely to outlast the Wessex fyrd.

If Alfred was to make any headway against this force, he would need to choose another approach very soon, for two reasons. First, the Wessex fyrd could only be kept in the field for a short period. Soon their supplies would dwindle, and the need for the men of Wessex to return to their fields and shops would begin to sap away the strength of the Saxon shieldwall. Second, Alfred had a very ominous foreboding about Guthrum's strategy. The Danish king had clearly chosen a position easily reached from the sea and well connected to the waterways of Wessex. Why would he choose what was clearly a naval base when he had come with land forces? Wareham was the perfect stronghold for a ship army. But where were the ships? Alfred knew that at any moment swarms of Viking longboats were likely to arrive, bringing thousands of Danish warriors, doubling or tripling Guthrum's army and killing any possibility the men of Wessex had of repelling this attack. Guthrum must be driven from Warehem immediately.

Alfred's desperation showed in the approach he finally chose. Once more, he paid the danegeld. Of course this wasn't the sort of tactic that could work over any extended period of time, but it was enough to extract Guthrum and his troop from Wareham. It should also be pointed out that, as disastrous as paying the danegeld had been for East Anglia and Mercia, Alfred's previous payment had been temporarily successful. It had seemed to buy a few years of peace.

Alfred clearly felt uneasy about this payment and made two extra demands as he negotiated the Viking withdrawal. First, the two armies exchanged hostages. A selection of Wessex men were taken into captivity by Guthrum, and Alfred chose an assortment of the most distinguished Danish noblemen to remain with him. These hostages were to ensure that the two kings honored their pledges to one another. If Guthrum failed to keep his end of the peace bargain, then Alfred would be free to exact his revenge on the Viking hostages, and vice versa.

Second, Alfred insisted that when Guthrum swore to withdraw his men, he must do so on the pagan relic that he held most dear, the holy ring of Thor. Fully aware that the Danish pagans had no respect whatsoever for the Christian God, Alfred was groping for something that might hold the Danish king to his vow. The ring of Thor, a large gold armband often worn on the chieftain's arm, was used by the Vikings when they swore oaths to one another. That Alfred would resort to a pagan relic was a clear sign of his deep desperation.

Alfred soon learned that an oath sworn to Thor meant no more to pagan Guthrum than it did to Christian Alfred. In the middle of one night, Guthrum cut the throats of all the Wessex hostages whom he had taken, mounted his entire army on horseback, and slipped out of Wareham. Completely ignoring his pledge to leave Wessex,

Guthrum rode hard and fast, straight to the city of Exeter, another easily fortified city sitting on the bank of the river Exe on the southern coast of Wessex. From Exeter, Guthrum could easily continue a lengthy campaign of conquest.

Alfred pursued the Danish troops with his own small mounted force, but he was too late. By the time he had reached Exeter, Guthrum had already taken the town, and the Danes were fattening themselves on the fresh provisions of their new fortress. Then, to make matters worse, Alfred received news that an enormous Viking fleet was moving along the southern coast of Wessex. Several thousand more Danish soldiers would soon be sailing up the river Exe to join Guthrum in his conquest of Wessex. With these troops, the Viking conquest of Wessex would be inevitable.

The fate of Wessex was all but sealed. Once this new navy joined forces with Guthrum, it would be impossible to drive the Danes from their freshly fortified stronghold in Exeter. Though Alfred's navy had been successful in repelling an earlier Viking fleet, that fleet had consisted of a mere seven ships. This new naval force was more than twenty times that size and far too large for Alfred to engage ship-to-ship. Only a miracle could prevent Wessex from being overrun by this pagan force.

And that was exactly what Alfred was given—a miracle. As the Viking longboats sailed along the southern coast, a terrible storm struck the fleet just off the shore of Swanage. Much like the great gale that was to deliver England from the invading Spanish Armada some seven centuries later, this tempest smashed the Danish ships to pieces on the perilously rocky coast of Dorset. Some accounts describe a thick mist that swallowed the ships and led them blindly to be dashed on the treacherous shores. In that one calamitous storm, 120 ships of the Viking fleet sank. Assuming that each of these ships was manned by an average of thirty men, this would have cost the Vikings thirty-six hundred men—a catastrophic loss. For Alfred, this storm was clearly nothing other than divine deliverance.

Once news of this disaster reached Guthrum, it was immediately obvious to the Danish king that his tactics must be altered. No longer intent on the conquest of Wessex, his aim now was to bargain for safe passage out of Alfred's kingdom, for himself and his men. Alfred, having already been burned by the Viking's duplicity in making vows for peace, was certainly dubious about how faithful Guthrum would be in keeping his vows. The Danish army's predicament gave the Wessex king enough reason to believe that Guthrum had no realistic opportunity for waging a campaign against Wessex. The two kings exchanged vows of peace once more. Alfred chose a great number of hostages from the Viking court but seems to have given no hostages of his own. Alfred did make one fairly significant concession to the raiding army, however, allowing them to remain in Exeter throughout the winter, all the way until the beginning of harvest, somewhere around the first week of August 877.

At first Guthrum proved true to his vows. At the beginning of harvest, he withdrew his troops from Exeter and marched north to

Mercia, where the puppet king Ceolwulf still ruled. Settling down in Mercian Gloucester, Guthrum then demanded of Ceolwulf that he divide up the Mercian kingdom, portioning out many of the Mercian shires to his own Viking noblemen for settlement. In doing so, Guthrum was following the example of Halfdan, who had similarly divided up Northumbria the previous year and had even begun tilling and harvesting the newly seized farmland.

In Gloucester, the Danes ravaged the countryside and drove out the Mercians, who were unprotected by their Viking-appointed king. Western Mercia was divided up into five boroughs and given to Guthrum's noblemen to settle and rule. Eastern Mercia, with the exception of Gloucester, remained under the authority of Ceolwulf, provided he continue to take his orders from Guthrum.

From Wessex, it was difficult for Alfred to interpret Guthrum's settlement in Mercia. On one hand, this new trend among the Viking kings of settling in permanent dwellings and beginning to farm the land might signal a dwindling interest in plundering and raiding, which might result in a welcome rest from the regular Viking raids. On the other hand, a Viking army settled in Mercia left a potential raiding army permanently poised on Wessex's northern border, capable of being reinforced and resupplied easily from the rear. This move might actually be a greater cause for alarm for Wessex. Alfred opted for this second interpretation. Clearly, the continuing existence of Wessex, the one Saxon kingdom left standing against the Danish invaders, constituted a significant threat to the Viking occupation of England.

Alfred was now familiar enough with Guthrum's tactics to know that another invasion could be expected at any moment, which meant that Guthrum must be closely watched. Though the fyrds of Wessex could not be kept permanently mobilized to wait for a Viking attack, Alfred was able to move a small troop of professional soldiers, a sort of advanced guard, to the royal estate at Chippenham on the banks of the river Avon in Wiltshire. With its close proximity to the border of Mercia, Chippenham was well situated for keeping an eye on Guthrum's troops and offered Alfred the ability to respond quickly to any suspicious Viking movements. If Guthrum began moving south again, Alfred would be ready to summon the fyrds of Wessex immediately and cut him off at the borders of Wessex.

Even though Alfred had learned much about his Viking opponent, Guthrum had learned more. First, Guthrum was now well practiced at striking in unexpected and undefended places by moving swiftly and silently through the territories of Wessex. This had been demonstrated with vicious clarity when he had crossed Wessex from north to south without raising any alarm and attacked the unsuspecting town of Wareham on the southern coast. Second, Guthrum had learned something of the Christian calendar and how it could be used by the Vikings to predict moments of weakness in the Saxon defenses. For instance, in AD 866, Ivar and Haldan had launched their attack on unsuspecting York on All Saints' Day, a day when the city, distracted by the celebration of the holiday, was least prepared to resist the attack.

While Guthrum seemed to be orchestrating the settlement of Mercia, he was also industriously bringing his army back up to full strength for another attack on Wessex. Bringing in new recruits from the continent and men from the Northumbrian campaign, the Danish king was soon able to make up for the thousands of men lost off the shores of Dorset when the one hundred twenty Viking ships were lost in the storm.

Within a few short months of leaving Exeter, Guthrum had his army fully reinforced and, despite the wintery season, drove south bent on conquest. Moving swiftly and completely unnoticed, Guthrum crossed the border of Wessex, breaking his vows of peace to Alfred at Exeter, and marched straight to Chippenham and straight toward Alfred. This time, Guthrum was not searching for a quick and easy raiding target, nor was he looking for a chance to draw the Wessex army out into open battle. This time, Guthrum aimed straight for Alfred, planning to decapitate the king in the hopes that without the powerful and unifying figure of Alfred, the kingdom would much more easily capitulate to Guthrum's rule.

Guthrum's attack was timed to coincide with the holiday of Twelfth Night, January 6, taking advantage of the distraction that the festivities of the holiday provided. Twelfth Night was the culmination of the Christmas season, a season that started with solemn reflection and prayer on Christmas Day and then slowly grew in mirth and merriment during the following twelve days, until the Twelfth Night, the eve of Epiphany, when the entire season ended with a great feast and much drinking of wassail.[1] It was a night of feasting and gift giving. It was to be celebrated by king and by peasant; no one was to be excluded. It was a night when, as a result of the Wessex merrymaking, the fortifications of Chippenham were left virtually unguarded, a moment well chosen by Guthrum.

Caught by surprise and possessing a force too small to withstand

[1] Wassail was a drink that derived its name from the Old English *wæs hæl*, meaning "be you well."

a full Viking raiding army, the citizens of Chippenham were easily overrun. The astonished Alfred was forced to retreat from Chippenham with his family and bodyguards to the countryside of Wiltshire until he could summon the fyrds and face Guthrum in combat.

But Guthrum moved too quickly. After seizing Chippenham, the Vikings convinced the ealdorman of Wiltshire, Ealdorman Wulfhere, to break his allegiance to Alfred and pledge his loyalty to Guthrum. Once Wulfhere had gone over to Guthrum, Alfred was cut off from the ordinary means of summoning the Wiltshire fyrd to battle, leaving Alfred defenseless.

Many other nobles of Wessex immediately sensed the impending annihilation of the last Saxon kingdom, so they followed the opportunistic example of Wulfhere, betraying their king and taking oaths of submission to Guthrum. Others, sensing the impossibility of the situation, took their cue from Burgred, the Mercian king, and fled to the European continent for refuge. It seemed inevitable that Wiltshire, Somerset, and Hampshire would soon be ravaged by the Viking raiders. The leadership of Wessex was in total disarray, leaving Alfred without any of the necessary means of communication to summon the fyrds of Wessex. Guthrum, without even fighting one pitched battle, had become the effective ruler of Wessex. And Alfred was forced to take his small group of faithful followers much deeper into hiding until a plan for striking back could be formed.

The following days would be the darkest Alfred would face, the true low point of his reign. Descriptions of Alfred during this time always emphasize the desperate solitude suffered by the king during these lonely months. He had been driven from his throne and betrayed by a number of his trusted friends. Those friends who had remained loyal in their friendship had become inaccessible to the wandering outcast king. Cut off from his throne, his court, and his armies, Alfred, betrayed and abandoned, wandered in the moors, wastelands, and fens of Wessex, moving into the marshes and woods of Somerset.

Refusing to abandon his kingdom, Alfred selected an ideal location from which he could continue to wage a campaign of guerrilla warfare resistance against Guthrum until Alfred had the opportunity to raise an army to face the Viking in all-out battle. Although these were easily the darkest days in Alfred's life, they also were to become the most famous. The stories of his persevering against the Vikings transformed King Alfred into Alfred the Great.

The story falls into a category that the modern ear can easily recognize and appreciate. From the legends of Robin Hood hiding out with his band of merry men in Sherwood Forest to the tales of men fighting in the underground French resistance during World War II, the modern listener has been well trained to be moved by the courageous nobility of continuing a campaign of resistance long after being driven into hiding. The seeming despair of a life of defiant resistance, while being hunted in one's homeland, captures the imagination and takes on a romantic hue. But this was not a category of story that the Anglo-Saxon ear was accustomed to hearing. To his contemporaries, Alfred's plight was an unqualified tragedy, utterly devoid of romanticism.

Understanding the weight of Alfred's plight requires a bit of knowledge concerning the ideals of the Anglo-Saxon society: the king sat
enthroned, not on a gaudy gold contraption that signaled the distance between his subjects and him, but on the mead bench, pushed
up to a long table, surrounded on all sides by his faithful warriors, the
men who stood next to him in the shieldwall throughout all of his
campaigns, his *thegns*. This table was piled high with fruits and veg-
etables from the farms of Wessex and laden with the flesh of roasted
boar, venison, and beef. An enormous horn was passed around the
table. The horn was gilded, crusted with gems, and overflowing with
mead—the sweet, intoxicating honey wine of the Anglo-Saxon warriors. An enormous fire in the center of the spacious room warmed
the raucous crowd late into the evening.

© iStock Photos

Throughout the evening, the band of men occasionally would grow silent when the thrumming of the lyre began and the poet-bard, the *scop*, began his singing. The song of the scop hovered somewhere between a haunting melody and rhythmic chant, with its steady meter strummed out on the lyre. The words of the scop brought back to life the legends of old at the same time that they immortalized the names of the men sitting in the hall. They told of the glory of battles fought bravely, whether won or lost. They spoke of the nobility of loyal thegns who stood resolutely by their lord no matter the cost. They spoke of the treachery of men who had eaten at the lord's table, taken his gifts, but then become unmanned at the sight of the enemy shieldwall and, filled with cowardice, turned their backs on their lord and ran from battle. They listed the names of the heroes and the cowards.

When the songs were finished, the king would give out gifts to his thegns. Generously, the gift giver would open up his treasure hoard and pour out his wealth to his loyal men. He gave gracious gifts of land with estates to noblemen. He gave farms and the profit that came with them. He gave horses, sacks of gold and silver coins, shields, helmets, swords, axes, necklaces, bracelets, and rings. This last category, the category of rings, came to epitomize the gifts of a gracious king. All Anglo-Saxon lords became known as "ring-givers." In return for these generous gifts, the men of the mead hall would pledge their complete devotion back to the ring-giver. If the king ever found himself in need of an army to face down an enemy, he would find that his gift giving had not been in vain. His loyal thegns would rise up and stand unflinching in the shieldwall to live or die with their ring-giver.

Years later, when Alfred had the leisure to write, he described feasting in the mead hall and the warm fellowship between the ring-giver and his thegns, the deep bond of *comitatus*, as the closest approximation he could make to life in heaven. This was life in the court of a king as it should be. Whenever something went wrong in Anglo-Saxon society, it was inevitably revealed as a failure to honor the most basic obligations pledged in the ring-giver's mead hall.

Those who were ostracized from this fellowship became the outcasts of Anglo-Saxon society—the men who had betrayed their lords or committed such heinous deeds that they had been driven from civilization. The Anglo-Saxon poem *Beowulf* opens with Grendel, a goblin-like descendent of Cain who prowls outside the great mead hall of Heorot, provoked to anger by the sounds of the comradery and fellowship of the ring-giver and his thegns within the hall. The monster Grendel walks the marshes and moors at night, listening to the voice of the scop chanting to the thrumming of his lyre, singing about Almighty God's creation of the earth. The song drives Grendel into a bloodthirsty rage, and he breaks into the mead hall that night to gorge on the flesh of the warriors sleeping there. For the ninth-century Anglo-Saxon, to be cast out of the mead hall was to be placed in the same company as Grendel, to be haters of God, haters of humanity.[2]

[2] Another poem, *The Wanderer*, describes the sorrows of a man who had served a lord who had died in battle. His ring-giver gone, the wanderer has been robbed of the hall fellowship that he once had with his lord. He, too, has been driven to wander the unforgiving wastelands of Anglo-Saxon England.

King Alfred had become a wanderer, a Grendel, prowling the wilds of Wessex. Betrayed and forsaken by many of his nobles, he turned to a close inner circle of family and friends who had remained loyal and followed him into hiding. This small band of warriors built a hidden camp for themselves in the far reaches of the Somerset levels at Athelney. From here, Alfred was able to continue his campaign against the Danes, by means of a sort of guerrilla warfare.

A large part of the success of this campaign came from the strategic location of his new hideout. A small piece of raised ground, guarded on one side by the river Tone and on all other sides by swamps, bogs, and flooding lakes, Athelney was approachable only by boat. William of Malmesbury, the early twelfth-century historian, described Athelney as an island, "though not an island of the sea." A scarce two acres of dry land rose up out of the marshy surrounds, but it was more than enough space to support the exiled king and his band of followers. With their stags, goats, and other wild beasts, these two wooded acres soon became Alfred's swampy fortress, a mead hall of the marshes and moors.

Alfred and his men spent the first wintery months of AD 878 at Athelney looking for opportunities to harass the Viking army as it attempted to occupy and consolidate power in its newly conquered territory. In small bands, the warriors of Wessex would creep out of the Somerset levels and seek Viking vulnerabilities. Where they encountered smaller parties of Danes, they attacked and slaughtered ruthlessly. Where they found larger Viking camps, they crept cautiously in, under cover of darkness, and quietly looted the camp of all its portable provisions. Those men of Wessex who had deserted their lord and pledged their allegiance to the pagan invaders also became targets of Alfred's frequent raids. Alfred wanted to make it clear to the people of Wessex that the king of the nation had not abandoned his land; he was still the ring-giver of Wessex, repaying his faithful thegns for their loyalty and punishing the traitors. Nearly all the great legends for which Alfred is still remembered refer to these few months as Alfred wandered the wilds of Wessex figuring out how to retake his kingdom.

Since many of these legends did not originate until several centuries later, they are probably not as reliable as the more contemporary accounts of Alfred's life. Admittedly, these later stories tend to be more fantastic. For instance, William of Malmesbury recounted how Alfred dressed himself up as a juggler and walked openly into the camp of the Danes, who, not recognizing him and thinking he was some sort of entertainer, welcomed him into their camp and demanded that he perform. The disguised king obliged them and performed for the Viking camp for several days, delighting them thoroughly. During this time he was able to walk freely through the camp, spying out their numbers, checking on their state of readiness, and collecting all the information necessary for forming his own strategies of attack.

Other legends emphasize how Alfred retained his care and compassion for the people of Wessex, despite the difficult lesson of humility that God was teaching him throughout his exile. In one account, as the king's men went out to fish one afternoon, the king and his wife stayed behind with a servant in their small dwelling on Athelney. A pilgrim came and begged bread of the king, who sent the servant to see how much food they had to spare. The servant returned to say that the family only had one loaf of bread and a bit of wine. Alfred immediately commanded that half of the loaf and half of the wine be given to the beggar, who took the gifts with gratitude. Of course, it was discovered later that the loaf of bread and the bit of wine had not been diminished at all, despite having been shared. That afternoon the fishing party returned with a miraculously bountiful catch. But the greatest surprise came that night when Saint Cuthbert, the great saint of Lindisfarne, appeared to Alfred to reveal that he had been the wandering pilgrim who had taken Alfred's bread and wine. Because of Alfred's generosity, Cuthbert would be the king's shield and friend and would watch over Alfred from then on. Cuthbert also gave Alfred a prophecy of his upcoming victory over the Danes, as well as the promise that Alfred would soon be the king of all Britain.

Most of these accounts first appeared in the twelfth or thirteenth centuries, leaving good reason to suspect that exaggerations have crept into the stories through many retellings of the tale. But the earliest legend of Alfred's months of wandering, and by far the most famous of all the stories of Alfred, is the story of Alfred and the cakes. The story appears in the tenth-century *Life of Saint Neot*, less than a century after Alfred's death. Neot had served as a monk in Cornwall, dying around AD 870, only a few years before Alfred came to Athelney.

According to the *Life of Saint Neot*, Alfred had heard Neot teach earlier in his life and was reflecting on a lesson that seemed to apply to his current hapless state. Neot had taught on Hebrews 12:6, in which the writer had quoted Proverbs 3:11–12, exhorting one not to despise the chastening of the Lord, because he chastises and scourges every son whom he receives. Alfred had this teaching in mind when he first arrived at Athelney, where he found an old swineherd's cottage. Alfred, completely alone at this point, sought refuge in this cottage where he was taken in and given food and shelter. The king did not divulge his true identity to the swineherd or his wife, however, and pretended to be a wandering commoner.

One afternoon as the swineherd was out in the pastures, Alfred sat in the cottage kitchen while the swineherd's wife busied herself with her household chores. As the king sat, he became absorbed in deep deliberation about his desperate plight. So lost in the contemplation of his own sorrows, Alfred failed to notice that a tray of cakes the peasant woman had placed into the oven to bake had begun to burn right in front of him. When the swineherd's wife saw the smoke of the burning cakes pour out of the oven and the distracted king sitting right in front of the oven doing nothing to save the cakes, she became furious and castigated Alfred for failing to turn the cakes. "Even though you are more than willing to eat the cakes when they come warm from the oven," she chided, "you still won't take the trouble to turn them when you see them burning!" Alfred, recalling the lesson he had been meditating on from Saint Neot, humbly accepted the correction and turned his attention to the baking cakes.

From his swampy refuge in Athelney, Alfred communicated through his continued attacks on the Danish camps, as well as on the traitors of Wessex, his undying determination to resist the Viking occupation, promising that he would one day soon rise up and drive the Danes from the borders of Wessex. The tales of Alfred's escapades comforted those who had remained loyal to the king throughout the occupation and discomforted those with Danish sympathies. As the legends of Alfred's resistance grew, they began to inspire other Wessex nobles to resist the Danish trespassers with greater resolve.

Toward the close of the winter of AD 878, as Alfred tended the cakes, the fyrd of Devon mobilized to fend off another invading Viking army. Ubbe, son of Ragnar Lothbrok, had sailed with a navy from Dyfed, in southwest Wales, to the northern coast of Devon. Ubbe had wintered in Dyfed, where in those few months he had slaughtered many of the Welsh natives. Now, hearing of Guthrum's advances in Wessex, Ubbe longed for a share in the booty and spoils of this last-standing Saxon nation.

Ubbe entered the Bristol Channel with twenty-three ships and landed on the shore of Devon. Odda, the ealdorman of Devon, led the Devon fyrd to the coastal town of Countisbury, where they prepared to intercept the newly arrived Viking army. The fyrd of Devon attempted to fortify Countisbury, but their work was cut short by the approaching Danish army long before it had been completed. Fortunately, despite the unfinished defenses, the craggy terrain that surrounded Countisbury provided a significant natural defense for the town. Because of the awkward situation of the town, Ubbe disliked the idea of a frontal assault on Odda's men. Instead, Ubbe opted to lay siege to the town, intent on starving the Saxons out.

Ubbe carried a legendary flag with him, which had been sewn by his three sisters for their father before his death. The flag was a triangular pennant with a border of tassels and the image of a raven sewn into the center. The raven symbolized Odin, the war god of the Vikings who gave the Danish warriors strength against their enemies. Odin was said to keep two ravens perched on his shoulders, one named Hugin, "thought," and the other Munin, "memory." These two birds flew off every morning at dawn, traveling throughout the world and bringing back news to whisper into Odin's ears. The presence of ravens wheeling and circling over a battlefield before a great combat, waiting to feast on the flesh of the fallen warriors, testified to Odin's special love for battles. The carrion birds devouring the dead was taken as a clear sign that Odin had accepted the carnage of the battle as a pleasing sacrifice.

The raven on the flag that Ubbe carried was said to have been imbued with magical qualities by his own sisters. Before a battle, if the Viking forces were to be victorious, the flag would prophesy that victory by fluttering and flapping, regardless of whether there was a breeze or not. If the battle was doomed to go against the Viking army, then the flag would hang still, no matter how fierce a gale blew against it.

As the men of Devon considered their situation, it was clear that they were fairly unprepared for a siege. Their preparations had been too hasty. In addition to not completing the fortifications of the town, they had not had time to stock Countisbury with the necessary provisions. Food supplies were already low, and there was no source of water within the town's defenses. Their future looked grim as they peered over the fortifications of Countisbury at the ominous raven banner, trying to discern whether the banner hung still or stood out, unfurled by a nonexistent breeze. And so, rather than wait until the situation became dire, the men of Devon decided to strike while they still had their strength, placing the Viking attackers on the defensive. It seemed to them that if one was doomed to die, it would be better to die while grasping for freedom, rather than while being starved into submission.

Bursting suddenly out of the besieged stronghold at dawn, they crashed into the astonished Viking army in an utterly unexpected frenzy. The Danish army was completely unprepared for this assault, and their front forces were overrun in an instant. Though outmanned, the sheer audacity of the attack gave the battle to the Saxon army. As the rampaging men of Devon cut through the astonished Viking front line, the rest of Ubbe's men had no choice but to turn and run. The savage predator had become the frantic prey. All the way to the coast of Devon, the Saxons chased the fleeing Vikings, hacking down virtually the entire Viking force. By the time the slaughter was finished, Ubbe and eight hundred of his men lay dead, a fresh feast for the ravens. Ragnar's banner, the raven flag, was carried proudly from the place of slaughter by Ealdorman Odda.

Many of the ealdormen of Wessex continued to put up a resistance against the Danish occupation. Men like Odda of Devon regularly proved to the Vikings that the Wessex resistance had not been entirely crushed. Had Alfred wanted to, he could have easily withdrawn from Athelney to a shire where the resistance to the Viking occupation was more established. Hampshire and Dorset seemed to be relatively untouched by the Viking invaders, and Alfred could have simply retreated to one of these royal estates. But the king refused to leave Somerset. Through his persistent raids on the unsuspecting Danes, he sought to remind Guthrum that the king of Wessex had not abandoned his nation. He also kept fresh in the minds of the people of Wessex that their king was soon to return, ready to repay the faithful and the unfaithful accordingly. But most of all, Alfred remained in Somerset because he insisted on staying as close to Guthrum as possible, shadowing all of his movements and observing his tactics. Alfred was studying his enemy, learning to hunt all over again.

CHAPTER 5

Whitsunday and the Battle of Edington

Now his passion and his resurrection have become our
Eastertide, since he has loosed us from the bondage of
the Devil, and our persecutors are submerged through
that holy baptism, just as Pharaoh and his men in the
Red Sea.

—ÆLFRIC, *Catholic Homilies* I. XXII

The months spent at Athelney gave Alfred
the opportunity to reflect on his defeats
and the various missteps he had made during the first few years of his reign. He could not be
faulted for his zeal or for his raw courage during that
brief period, but he began to realize he had lacked
the cunning necessary to outwit such a battle-savvy
opponent as Guthrum. The only great victory he had
experienced to date had been the glorious triumph
at Ashdown. But that victory had come largely as
a result of an entirely accidental ruse the Saxons
had played on the Vikings. Hiding half of Wessex's

forces until after the battle was well under way had been a brilliant and effective trick. But it had been an entirely unintended stratagem, whereas the pagan warriors seemed capable of deceiving and manipulating the Saxons almost at will. They could lure the gullible Christians into almost any treaty and then break it without a second thought. They could exchange hostages as a great show of good intentions and then slit the throats of the innocents a moment later.

Not only were the Vikings significantly more cunning, they were also far more logistically effective. They could successfully organize incredibly complex troop movements, sending one army over land and another by sea to meet at a prearranged point—hundreds of miles deep into their enemy's territory and weeks into the future. Even more astonishing, they could execute these troop movements through hundreds of miles of Wessex territory, with Wessex only beginning to notice when one of her great cities had already been seized and fortified against her. If Alfred was to be victorious against Guthrum, he would need the ability to defeat the Danish king at his own game.

Additionally, if Alfred was to make a stand against the Viking conquerors, then he would need to find a way of instilling a deeper sense of principle in the Wessex ealdormen. Across Britain, the Vikings had thoroughly exploited all the character defects in the Saxon leadership. By capitalizing on these weaknesses, the Danes had easily divided the Saxon nobility and weakened Britain's resistance to their conquest. For instance, when the sons of Ragnar Lothbrok invaded Northumbria, they struck just as the nation had fallen into a vicious civil war between Osberht and Ælle, two contenders for the Northumbrian throne. The bitter infighting of the Northumbrian leadership had left the nation defenseless and ripe for the picking.

When the Danes received danegeld from King Burgred in Mercia and King Edmund in East Anglia, they sensed a weakness begging to be exploited in the rulers. They returned soon after with such a show of strength that both Mercia and East Anglia immediately crumbled with very little military resistance.

If Alfred was to defeat his enemy, he needed to teach his noblemen to be cunning but principled, crafty as serpents and innocent as doves. His men had to become deathly shrewd and able to trump the Vikings in guile and deception. But at the same time, they had to sense the deep need for leaders who understood the principles of nobility. They had to despise the nearsighted purchasing of today's peace with tomorrow's freedom and see it for the cowardice that it was. They had to prefer to die a gory death in a hopeless combat than to live a craven life having betrayed the king and the people of Wessex. The pagan invaders could not have conquered a nation led by noblemen who understood true nobility.

Living these few months under Guthrum's authority had already taught a good deal of this second lesson. The continued looting and pillaging of the Wessex shires, the ransacking of the churches and farms, the raping and kidnapping, had all exacted a heavy toll from the people of Wessex. Anyone who had thought that life under the Vikings would be preferable to a campaign against them had been thoroughly corrected. It was now clear that freedom would have been worth continuing to fight for.

The cunning that Alfred had lacked, he began to learn in Athelney. From here he tracked the Viking king, learning to predict his movements and how to react effectively and counter his tactics.

He practiced moving his own men unseen throughout Guthrum's newly occupied territory. He also began to construct an effective but entirely secret network of communication between himself and the ealdormen who were still loyal to him among the shire fyrds of Wessex.

By Easter, Alfred had constructed his own hidden fortress at Athelney, guarded by a watery seclusion and the few faithful thegns who had followed the king into hiding. A mile northeast of Athelney, Alfred was able to post a lookout on Burrow Mump, a prominent peak rising several hundred feet above the desolate surrounds that offered, on a clear day, a view for hundreds of miles in all directions. From here, Alfred could easily track from afar any movement of the Danish troops, offering him even greater opportunities to harass Guthrum's uneasy troops.

For Guthrum the situation had become surprisingly more and more difficult. He had been a master at commanding an invading army, but occupying a foreign nation while being savagely harassed by a resolute underground force was a skill in which he was terribly unpracticed. To truly control Wessex, Guthrum needed to conquer Alfred and his small band of guerrilla warriors, who seemed to be everywhere and nowhere. Fighting this ubiquitous menace required that virtually all of his troops be held back either in the shire of Somerset searching out Alfred or in Wiltshire protecting Guthrum's base at Chippenham. But this left the southern shires of Dorset and Hampshire untouched by the Viking occupation, as well as the other far reaches of Wessex. Alfred's continued attacks from Athelney were keeping Guthrum from driving his conquest home. The one chance Guthrum had of finding assistance had been lost when the ealdorman of Devon, Odda, had routed the newly arrived Ubbe and his men at the failed siege of Countisbury.

Alfred realized it was critical that the southern shires remain free from the desperate grip of Guthrum. Had Ubbe been successful in his earlier invasion of Devon, the fate of Wessex would have been sealed. Therefore, even though it would have been very helpful if the strong Saxon fyrds of Dorset and Devon were to come to the north to help wage battle against Guthrum, it was necessary that they remain at home to defend the coasts of Wessex. This left Alfred depending on the men of Somerset, Wiltshire, and Hampshire to fill out the army he was secretly gathering. The ealdorman of Wiltshire, Wulfhere, had betrayed Alfred, however, and pledged his faithfulness to Guthrum. Gathering the men of Wiltshire to his side without the leadership of the shire's ealdorman would not be easy for Alfred. But Wulfhere's duplicity had been a betrayal of his own people every bit as much as it had been a betrayal of the Wessex king. During the months since Guthrum's attack on Chippenham, the men of Wiltshire had come to loathe their perfidious lord, a loathing that made them all the more passionately devoted to their outcast king and his cause.

In the middle of the month of April, when the men of Wiltshire received a secret communication from Alfred summoning them for battle, they received the call to arms with intense joy and thanksgiving at the chance to rid themselves of the pagan oppressors. The call was passed on to Somerset and Hampshire as well, shires whose ealdormen had remained faithful to Alfred throughout Guthrum's conquest. At the village level, the leading men regularly gathered together at a meeting called the "folk-moot," where local business was conducted and word from the ealdormen and king was regularly announced. Additionally, each village would send leading men to meet at the "shire-moot," a similar meeting convened to conduct shire business. These governing bodies provided the means for Alfred to summon the men of Wessex to battle easily. These bodies also provided natural assembly points for each village and shire.

As the countryside of Wessex shook off the death grip of the English winter, as the frost and bone-biting chill fled from the climbing sun and lengthening days, as the floor of the woods sprang to life with the budding of the daffodils and bluebells, as all of nature declared with finality the death of winter, every man of Wessex capable of carrying a weapon into combat began his preparations for one more perilous clash with the Viking hordes. The following days were filled with the necessary task of equipping themselves for the fight, a task made all the more difficult by the need to hide the preparations from the Danish occupiers. Swords and axe-blades were sharpened, chain byrnies mended, spears fashioned, and hearts hardened. The message that had been passed on commanded the fyrds to gather at Egbert's stone on the southern border of Wiltshire, east of Selwood Forest.

Timing was, of course, critical to the success of Alfred's plans. It was essential that the Wessex shires move swiftly and quietly to this meeting point, giving the Danes as little forewarning as possible. But there was an additional significance to the timing of Alfred's summons. The Vikings had regularly exploited the Christian holy calendar to strike the Saxons at moments when they were least prepared. Now Alfred, in a perfectly poetic irony, chose to use the Christian calendar against the pagan invaders and appointed Whitsunday as the day of meeting. Whitsunday, or Pentecost, comes seven weeks after Easter and commemorates the descent of the Holy Spirit onto the disciples of Jesus, empowering them to preach the kingdom of Christ throughout Israel and beyond.

By gathering the fyrds of Wessex at Egbert's stone on Whitsunday, Alfred drew from the sense of hope and divine purpose that the season from Easter to Whitsunday regularly evoked among the Christian churches. By this point, most of the men of Wessex had not seen the king for some time and had only been aware of his continued resistance against the Vikings through the legends and fanciful tales about the king's exploits that were being circulated throughout the Wessex villages. When the noblemen and their assembled armies finally gathered together at Egbert's stone and saw the king in person, it was, as one of Alfred's friends and biographers put it, as if the king had been restored to life after a terrible tribulation.

Despite the deep joy of seeing their king once more, as well as Alfred's corresponding elation in finding that he still commanded an undying faithfulness from the warriors of Wessex, there was little time for celebration at this meeting. The gathering at Egbert's stone turned quickly to the grim business at hand. An army of four to five thousand men, as Alfred had assembled for this Whitsunday reunion, could not be kept in the field without quickly attracting Guthrum's attention. In fact, it was entirely likely that even then, as they welcomed their seemingly resurrected king, Guthrum had already received word of this new threat and was assembling his own forces for an attack. Alfred wasted little time in giving his orders to the commanding ealdormen. They were to spend one night at Egbert's stone, and early on the following morning, they would break their camp and immediately march north, straight toward Guthrum's stronghold in Chippenham. On the following day, the Wessex armies marched as far as Iley Oak on the edge of Warminster, where they made camp once more. By now Alfred had received word that Guthrum, too, was on the move.

Guthrum had indeed been alerted to the gathering fyrds of Wessex and had ordered his armies to prepare to intercept the approaching Saxon throng. Though the Viking king was surprised to hear that the outcast ruler had suddenly surfaced, and even more astonished to learn that Alfred was leading a full-strength army out of the Wessex wastelands, there was a corresponding relief that he would finally be able to face the king in open battle instead of endlessly searching the fens of Wessex for the elusive warrior. Guthrum hastily summoned his men to Chippenham and then, once a large enough force had been mustered, led them south to intercept the Wessex fyrds. After a day's march south, Guthrum took the hill fortress of Bratton Camp, an Iron Age fortification whose earthen ramparts still stood, offering the Viking army an easily defended outer wall. More importantly, Bratton Camp offered a strategic position for cutting off the approach to Chippenham.

Bratton Camp sat fourteen miles south of Chippenham and two short miles from the Saxon village of Edington, the site of one of

Alfred's royal estates. Because of Bratton Camp's proximity to this village, the descriptions of the battle that would soon ensue would regularly refer to this as the battle of Edington. The ancient fortress of Bratton Camp sat on the northern edge of a long, flat ridgeline that terminated at the Bratton Downs. On three sides, the Danish camp was protected by a steeply dropping slope, whose incline was much too steep to serve as an approach during an attack. This left the southern edge of the camp as the only possible access, where the ridgeline offered a broad and easy path to the camp.

Though the ancient fortifications could have been defended should Alfred have decided to lay siege to Guthrum, the lack of any water supply within the old earthen ramparts made Bratton Camp a less-than-ideal fortification for resisting a prolonged siege. Had Guthrum wanted to wait Alfred out, he would have been better off waiting in Chippenham where the fortifications, provisions, and water supply enabled the Vikings to be more prepared for a long siege. Instead, Guthrum, confident in his ability to crush this last bit of Wessex's resistance, had chosen to march his men to Bratton Camp because he wanted to cut off Alfred's advance north and force the king to face him in battle on the open fields before Edington.

By the time Alfred reached Iley Oak, he had already received word that Guthrum had left the walls of Chippenham and had begun moving south to halt the advance of the fyrds. There was now no chance of simply laying siege to the Vikings in Chippenham in order to bargain for their surrender and peaceful withdrawal. Like the Vikings who had already settled down in Northumbria and Mercia and had begun planting crops, Guthrum was no longer interested in a quick seizing of the danegeld of Wessex; he wanted to rule the kingdom unrivaled.

From Iley Oak, it would only take a short march the next morning before the Wessex warriors reached Bratton Camp, where the shieldwall of the Danes stood waiting for them. Thus, when the Saxon men laid down to sleep that night, under the early summer sky, they slept the uneasy sleep of men who knew they would face combat in the morning. That evening found the Saxon camp occupied with the business of preparing for battle—the last sharpening of the blades, a final checking over of the armor, and extended periods of private prayers. Many of the soldiers would also take a bit of time to bury or hide any wealth they might be carrying. By burying their coins, they robbed the enemy of the chance to grow wealthy from the plunder of the battlefield, should the Saxons fall in the fight. As they hid their wealth, however, they were sure to mark their hiding spots well so that, if they were to survive the morning's combat, they would be able to locate and reclaim their small hoards.

Early the next morning, the Saxon warriors were roused by the unrelenting revelry of spring—from the cacophony of birds' songs that sounded in the trees above them announcing the break of day to the cruelly early spring sunrise that set the horizon on fire and shone brightly in the squinting eyes of the still-groggy wakers. By mid-May, the horizon was already blazing at five o'clock in the morning. Shortly, the dew-drenched warriors had risen, eaten a final breakfast, and begun their last solemn march north. Within a few short hours, they were drawing near to Bratton Camp, the Viking stronghold.

Curiously, modern visitors of this battle site will notice that on the steep western slope, just below the still-discernable earthen ramparts of the old fortress, is another enormous white horse, cut into the hillside. Standing around one hundred feet tall, the Westbury White Horse towers over the valley below. The design of this horse, though definitely more horse-like than the elegantly iconic white horse that watched over the battle of Ashdown, seems much more static and stiff.

Much of the stiffness of the shape of the Westbury horse comes from the fact that in the early twentieth century the entire horse was filled in with concrete and then painted. Before the arrival of the concrete, the Westbury horse had been a chalk horse, whose image had been cut into the hillside in 1778 by George Gee. However, Gee had been motivated to design this new horse by another, older horse that had already been cut into the hillside. Apparently Mr.

Gee did not feel that this older horse looked horse-like enough and replaced it with the figure now frozen in concrete below the ruins of Bratton Camp. The age of this earlier horse is difficult to discern. The earliest printed description of it can be dated as far back as only a century befor Mr. Gee. It is also possible that it dates back as far as the Anglo-Saxon period. Eighteenth-century depictions of the earlier figure reveal an image too Anglo-Saxon in shape for the idea to be dismissed easily. It is difficult to answer this question with anything more than speculation, but the appearance of a white horse on possibly two of Alfred's most renowned battlefields is surely a strange coincidence.

As Alfred led the Saxon army up the ridgeline, the fortified ruins of Bratton Camp finally came into view. In front of those ditchwork defenses stood the Viking army, already formed in their menacing shieldwall, hungrily beckoning the Wessex king forward to try one last time to drive them from his borders. Alfred halted the march and gave a hasty command to his men to draw their weapons and take their places in the Saxon shieldwall. As the Wessex soldiers clamored into their attacking formation, the king earnestly exhorted his men. He oversaw the formation of the wall, ensuring the shields of the front line were tightly overlapped and firmly held.

But knowing that the strength of the shieldwall depended on more than strength of grip, he sought to strengthen their courage and resolve with his words. He reminded them of their vows to their ring-giver and exhorted them to stand true to their bold promises.

He derided the cowardice of every man who had ever run from a shieldwall. He extolled those faithful thegns who preferred to lie slain on the field of slaughter rather than to be found among those who broke the shieldwall and ran. He promised wealth and glory to the men who stood resolutely by his side in the coming onslaught. And he urged them to place their deepest trust in their merciful and mighty God. After thus exhorting his men, Alfred locked himself into the tightly woven shieldwall and advanced with his men toward the gore-hungry Viking army.

Neither the Vikings nor the Saxons brought any sort of mounted force to the combat, and so there would be no cavalry charge. Both armies tended to use archery only for hunting and left their bows behind when coming into battle. This meant that the shieldwalls had to move quite close before any actual combat began. But there was another sort of warfare that began long before any blows were landed—the psychological warfare of intimidation. Even as the Wessex army first began to form their shieldwall, they could hear the Viking warriors beating out a chilling challenge, rhythmically striking their spears upon the rims of their shields, drumming out an ominous cadence that rolled down the ridgeline and summoned the Saxons to the place of slaughter.

Once their arrangement was complete and the Wessex shieldwall began to advance toward the pagan host, they were greeted by an eruption of screaming taunts and jeers. This signaled the start of the first formality of the battle, the *flyting*—the exchange of insults, an element well practiced by the Viking warriors. The Danish throng began to shout across the open ground between the two closing shieldwalls, screaming out their prophecies of a coming Viking victory. They recounted their exploits throughout the already conquered shires of Wessex and related their opinion of the Saxon women. They promised to feed the flesh of their fallen adversaries to the hungry ravens circling overhead, the emissaries of their god Odin. For King Alfred, all the hopes of Wessex depended now on his ability to keep the Saxon shieldwall bound tightly together and the courage of his thegns resolute and unflagging. He urged his men on with confident defiance, spurning the Viking taunts.

Once the two lines had come within forty paces of one another, they were vulnerable to spear attacks. Although most of the Anglo-Saxons left their bows at home when coming to war, each Saxon warrior would have been expected to bring a small collection of spears. One of these spears, slightly longer than the rest, was reserved for thrusting once the two shieldwalls had made contact. The rest of the spears, up to three in number and held in the shield hand, were brought for throwing while the enemy was still some distance away. These throwing spears were slightly smaller than the thrusting spear and had descended from the older Roman *pilum*. They measured around six feet in length and were fitted with a very long and slender barbed iron head.

As the two shieldwalls closed on one another, men from the rear ranks began to lob their spears over the heads of the forward shieldwall and into the approaching lines of Viking soldiers. In a moment, the sky was black with Viking and Saxon javelins, each spear (or "gar" according to the Anglo-Saxon tongue) traced a slow and gentle path through the early summer sky. The paths of the spears seemed at first almost comically slow and clumsy. Each spear weighed less than two pounds and moved so slowly that a man could easily side-step the missile's fall or catch the spear with his bare hand before it hit the ground.

But the synchronized launch of thousands of spears so clouded the sky with the plummeting darts that a man's upward-turned eyes were overwhelmed instantly and could not even begin to pick out the individual spear that was marked for his forehead. But even if a man was able to identify the spear that was aimed at him, if he was in a forward position in the shieldwall, then his body was so tightly pinned between the bodies of his comrades that he had no possibility of sidestepping the falling spear point.

Down the spears rained on the two bands of warriors. Despite the light weight of these missiles, by the time they reached impact they had gathered enough momentum that they would drive straight through the torso of a grown man and emerge on the other side. If the doomed soldier was wearing a mail byrnie, the head of the spear could still split the armor and sink four to five inches into his flesh. When the soaring flock of spears landed on the shieldwall below, a cacophony of bellows and screams erupted as the mortally wounded fell to the ground thrashing, spitted by the slender shafts of ash. Of course, many of the men managed to block the incoming spears with their raised shields. But the falling shaft still carried enough momentum that it would drive though the wooden shield and stick up to a foot out the other side, frequently splitting the arm that held the shield as well.

The spear head was designed with a barb that made it impossible to pull the spear back out once the spear had driven through the linden planks of a shield. This meant that a man who had successfully blocked an oncoming spear with his shield (without severely damaging his own arm in the process) now had an immovable six-foot shaft projecting from his shield, rendering his shield so awkward to wield that it became useless and had to be discarded. As the two armies spent their throwing spears, the front ranks of the two shieldwalls were weakened. The dead and wounded dropped to the ground and were swiftly replaced from behind. Those who had lost their shields moved to the back of the shieldwall and readied their axes for the next stage of combat.

Still the two shieldwalls drew ever closer to one another. Even as the dead fell all around them, Alfred worked hard to urge his men forward with unflagging determination and courage. The Vikings, for their part, continued working on intimidating and demoralizing the Saxon line. If a hole could be created in the Wessex shieldwall before the lines had even met, then the Vikings could easily rip through the Wessex ranks at the moment the two shieldwalls collided, and the battle would be a rout. But as long as the Saxons resolutely held their formation tightly together, as long as men swiftly and willingly stepped in to fill every gap created by a fallen soldier, then the Wessex shieldwall would be impenetrable, and the Saxons would stand a good chance of dominating the place of slaughter.

But the Vikings still had one more deadly weapon to launch at the Saxons before the opposing shieldwalls collided. When the two forces were still twenty paces apart from one another, small bands of maniacally crazed Viking warriors burst forward from behind the Danish shieldwall and sprinted straight at the Saxon ranks. These lunatic bands were the Viking berserkers, the shock force of the Danish army. They were Odin's special devotees, men who prepared

for battle with a hypnotic ritual dance that drove them into a mind-
less, bloodthirsty frenzy.

Before a battle, these men danced in small circles and, through great
concentration and an occasional hallucinogenic mushroom, worked
their minds into a murderous craze, a mental state they referred to as
berserkergang. They painted their faces to appear like hideously grotesque
wild beasts and went either nude or wore only the skins of bears or
wolves. They believed that as their minds were
overcome with the bloodlust frenzy and they
entered the *berserkergang*, the spirits of wild
beasts possessed them and gave them the
strength of wolves and bears.[1]

For Guthrum, the real advantage of
deploying the berserker bands was not in
their ability to inflict significant casualties on
the opposing force but rather in their ability to
instill terror in the front ranks of the opposing army as the two forces approached. The
spectacle of a few dozen maniacal nude warriors slashing bloodthirstily through the
Saxon shieldwall created a powerful sensation
of despair in the Wessex troop. And a shieldwall filled with desperation was easy to break.
Thus, the attack of the berserkers, sprinting
straight into the Saxon ranks in a shrieking
murderous delirium, hacking and slashing, was
calculated to weaken the Saxon resolve just
moments before the two shieldwalls clashed,

[1] One description of the
onset of the berserker
rage recounted how
the trance began with
shivering, chattering
of teeth, and a chill all
over the body. Then the
warrior's face flushed
with color and began to
swell as he was carried
away by the rage. At
this point, the berserker
received superhuman
strength and could bite
through a shield or cut
down anything in his
path. So relentless was
the murderous rage
that berserkers could
be severely wounded
innumerable times
without noticing that
they had been so much
as scratched.

like an artillery salvo softening up the resistance just before the landing of troops on an enemy beachhead.

The shrieking bands of berserkers crashed into the Wessex shieldwall in a maniacal frenzy. But, contrary to Guthrum's hopes, the Saxon warriors were less than terrified by the streaking Danes. The naked Northmen, convinced that the animal spirits that possessed them had rendered them invincible, were sorely disappointed when the front rank of the Wessex force stood resolute and unflinching. Within seconds, the wave of berserkers lay impaled on ashen spears or dismembered by Saxon axes, and the Saxon wall stood unbroken and more confident than before.

With one last shout, Alfred, the ring-giver of Wessex, urged his men to be true to their vows and fired their hearts with courage as the Saxon line braced for the coming impact. Across the shrinking gap between the two armies, the last of the Viking taunts and the various pagan invocations of Odin swirled in the air and soon turned into one indiscernible gore-hungry red-faced maniacal shriek. In that deafening roar of bloodcurdling shouting and horrific howling the two shieldwalls crashed into one another.

Spears cracked, shields split, axes crashed down, cleaving helm and skull. The front ranks did their best to hold the protective wall of shields tightly together while attempting to drive hard against the opposing wall. The next few ranks raised their spears overhead and looked for opportunities to drive their shafts down between the overlapped shields of the opposite wall. Spears searched and probed, looking between the linden shields for an inch of unguarded flesh to stab or slice. The keen eyes of the spearmen hunted vigorously for an uncovered shoulder, an exposed thigh, or an unwary skull.

Wherever a faltering or inattentive defense could be found, there the spearmen drove their deadly shafts. First they gashed open exposed limbs. Then as the wounds began to add up and the pain and blood loss weakened the fey warrior, his shield dropped lower and lower and his vital organs became vulnerable to attack. With deadly cunning the spearmen worked on the defenses of one another's shieldwalls, like wolves singling out the easiest kills. Then, as the men from the front ranks were cut down by the constantly stabbing spear tips, the shieldwall would weaken momentarily. At that moment, the opposing shieldwall could drive hard in the hopes that an opening had been cut in the enemy wall, but if the fallen warrior's place was filled quickly and the drive repulsed, then the game would begin again.

Throughout the course of the morning, the two bloodied armies contested for possession of the place of slaughter. The Viking host was grimly determined to hew a sacrifice for the beaks and talons of the circling ravens, a gory gift to their ravenous war god Odin. But the Christian army fought no less determinedly, having now come to understand what the consequences would be if they were to lose this last opportunity to drive the pagan invaders from their nation. For the better part of that day, the combat raged on. Often the two shieldwalls would separate for a moment or two, giving the men a brief respite. Then, once vaguely refreshed, the two walls would clash once more, probing and searching for the weak link— a softness in the shieldwall—where the opposing ranks could be driven apart and the enemy forces routed. But victory at the battle of Edington would not be seized easily.

The battle raged on well into the afternoon, after both sides had already paid dearly. As both shieldwalls became severely depleted by the casualties of the combat and as an intense exhaustion began to weigh the fatigued warriors down, it was clear that the determining factor of the battle would be a simple matter of discovering who had more endurance. The sprint had become a marathon. The two forces were evenly matched in numbers and strength, so the victor would be decided by whichever side was willing to continue putting everything into the shieldwall for the longest time.

At some point late in the afternoon, the ferocity of the Viking assault began to flag and lose its bite. They did not care for the land of Wessex nearly as much as the men of Wessex, and so, in the end, they were not able to outlast the determination and passion of the shieldwall Alfred commanded. Soon the decline in intensity of the Danes could be felt by the shieldwall of Wessex as it began to require less effort to hold its ground against the raiding army. The sudden realization that the Viking force was weakening galvanized the Saxon troop, which renewed its determination and sent them pushing harder and more resolutely against the Viking defenses. With spirits fired for victory, the men of Wessex strained against the stretching and faltering Danish lines.

Finally, the Viking shieldwall broke, and the full fury of the Anglo-Saxon warriors poured through the Viking ranks with such a wild ferocity that Odin himself would have cringed. With readied axes and swords, the men of Wessex cut a swath of carnage through the pagan ranks that made the Viking berserkers look like gentle lambs in comparison. Having lost the ability to hold together the shieldwall formation, the Viking ranks became governed by chaos and bedlam. Some of the Danes, knowing their doom was upon them, turned and fled from the battlefield, but most continued to fight on in smaller bands.

No longer was the fighting a coordinated affair of long rows of overlapping shields and well-aimed spear thrusts. Now the combat turned to the mad havoc of sword and axe fighting. Each man stood or fell by the quickness and power of his blows and the agility of his feet. But as it gradually became clearer to the Danes that the battle had been lost to them, they no longer fought with the goal of holding the place of slaughter but rather for a chance to find room to bolt from the battlefield, happy to escape with their lives.

At this point it was clear that the fyrds of Wessex had put the Danish army to rout, and they began to feel again the old temptation to relax their attack, to turn away from the bloody battle to nurse their own wounds and begin enjoying their victory. But Alfred had learned the hard way how failing to press on even after a clear victory could easily turn the tide of the battle against him. The king, who once earned for himself the title "the wild boar" for his rampaging combat at the battle of Ashdown, was unrelenting in his attack. He fought on fiercely and unrelentingly. Those Danes who still stood on the battlefield trying to save their own lives, if not the battle, were soon surrounded and overpowered by Wessex soldiers, who cut them down mercilessly. On they fought, until the fields of Edington were drenched with Danish blood, and not one Viking remained standing on the place of slaughter.

Once the enemy had been driven entirely from the battlefield, Alfred ordered the Saxon forces to chase the Danes who had escaped. All through the late afternoon and into the night, the Wessex soldiers pursued the fleeing Vikings, savagely slaying all whom they found. In the gloaming of the early summer evening, the Saxons searched through fen and forest for their prey, following the reckless footprints, the bloody tracks, and the tortured moanings of the panicked Danes. Once more the roles had reversed, and Alfred was again the hunter, tracking his prey in the wilds of Wessex. Guthrum was the prey, slinking silently through the night back to the safety of his stronghold in Chippenham.

Guthrum managed to find his way back to his fortress that night, eluding the hunters of Wessex and slipping back into Chippenham before dawn the next morning. By sunrise, a handful of the surviving Danes had joined Guthrum and, along with the forces the Viking king had left behind to protect his temporary capital, they began to fortify the walls of Chippenham in a desperate attempt to prepare for the coming Saxon siege.

Their preparations were none too soon. Within hours of daybreak, Alfred had positioned his army all about Guthrum's feebly defended walls, cutting off all chance of escape. Once he had ensured that his siege of the walls of Chippenham was sufficiently orchestrated, Alfred turned his remaining troops to the land surrounding Chippenham, laying to waste what had become over the past few months a Viking settlement. Any captured Danes were slaughtered immediately, and the horses and cattle the Vikings had pastured outside the city walls were all seized.

Within the walls of Chippenham, the scene began to look desperate. The Viking strength had been cut to ribbons at the battle of Edington. The few surviving warriors who had managed to return from the slaughter were wounded and exhausted. The reserve troops that Guthrum had kept behind at Chippenham were too few to resist the Saxon throng outside the gate. And if the predicament of the Danes was not already dire, the Chippenham fortress had just begun to reach the end of its winter stores, as the harvest was still many months away and the fortress had not yet been sufficiently supplied to hold out for any length of time. It is not surprising that the historical account of Guthrum's plight from the *Anglo-Saxon Chronicle* described the Danes at this point as "terrified by hunger, cold, and fear."

Alfred and his men waited hungrily at the gates of Chippenham for an entire fortnight, looking for their opportunity to strike and definitively end the Viking excursion into Wessex. As the impossibility of his situation became clear, Guthrum finally resigned himself to pleading for Alfred's mercy and seeking out terms of surrender. After fourteen days of siege, Guthrum sent a message to Alfred begging for an opportunity to abandon Chippenham and remove his men from Wessex entirely. In his desperation, the Viking king offered to give to Alfred as many hostages as the Saxon king requested and promised to let Alfred choose the hostages. Additionally, Guthrum offered to leave without taking any Wessex hostages with him.

All the Danish ruler requested was that he and his men might be allowed to leave Wessex alive. An invading Viking king had never before offered this type of one-sided peace treaty, one-sided in the favor of the Saxons. But the battle of Edington had suddenly reduced Guthrum to groveling for his life.

Alfred was prepared to grant Guthrum the mercy for which he begged. Up to this point, the Wessex king had been cruel and harsh in pressing home his victory. This brutality had been necessary to ensure that he not allow the Saxon victory to slip from his grasp.

Now that his victory was sure and his throne was securely established once again, it was time to make room for mercy. Alfred sent the Danish emissary back to Guthrum with the good news that the king of Wessex was prepared to allow the Danes to quit the town of Chippenham peacefully, though Alfred made one significant addition to the terms of Guthrum's surrender.

In granting Guthrum's desperate request, Alfred was being much more gracious to Guthrum than the Danish conquerors had ever been to the various Saxon kings who had surrendered to the Viking raiding armies. In East Anglia, Ubbe Ragnarsson and Ivar the Boneless had mockingly filled King Edmund with arrows until he bristled like a hedgehog, and then beheaded the Christian king. In Northumbria, Ivar and Halfdan had ritually sacrificed King Ælle to the Norse god Odin in the gruesome spectacle of the blood eagle. If this Guthrum were to be treated as the Viking kings had previously treated their conquered foes, if this humbled Danish king were to receive measure for measure, he would be cruelly executed before the Saxon troops for their evening's entertainment, and all the captured Viking soldiers would be quickly beheaded. Alfred was determined to make his victory clear to the vanquished Dane in terms that the Vikings would understand, but he also wanted to set a new example with this victory.

And so, just as Ivar and Halfdan had once sacrificed the conquered King Ælle to their god in the barbaric blood eagle ceremony, Alfred insisted that Guthrum must likewise be given over to the God of his conquerors. If Guthrum refused, the doom of the Viking soldiers was certain, and they would never leave Chippenham alive. Rather than the sadistic human sacrifice that Odin required, however,

Alfred insisted that Guthrum be handed over to the Christian God by the bloodless ceremony of baptism. The Vikings could go free from Chippenham if Guthrum was given to the triune God of Christianity through Christian baptism in the name of the Father, Son, and Holy Ghost.

Throughout the ninth century, baptism had often played an important role in the negotiations between pagan and Christian rulers. Numerous Viking rulers leading campaigns in northern Europe had already received Christian baptism in the hopes that the adoption of the Christian faith would improve their ability to bargain with the Carolingian rulers. Of course the effectiveness of this practice remains a debatable matter. Many of the pagans receiving baptism proved to have undertaken the ceremony with less-than-noble intentions. The seed sown in the hearts of the Viking rulers often fell on stony places or amidst choking thorns.

Certainly, Alfred had good reason to be suspicious of oaths taken by Danes. He had already seen the Vikings break countless vows, vows made before the Christian God, vows made to their own gods, even vows made with Viking hostages given as guarantees. None of these had proved sure. How could Alfred think that Guthrum would suddenly begin to respect the vow of Christian baptism? Nevertheless, after a siege of one fortnight, this is what Alfred demanded of Guthrum: not only was Guthrum required to take Alfred's God as his own, but King Alfred was to stand as Guthrum's new godfather at this christening. Guthrum accepted Alfred's terms immediately and swore to Alfred that he would honor the terms of this treaty, offering to Alfred his pick of the surviving Danish noblemen for hostages to guarantee this vow.

With the battle of Edington won and the army of Guthrum decisively conquered, it would seem that the time for Alfred to begin his celebrations had come. Surely this hard-won peace deserved a great feast in the mead hall of one of Alfred's great royal estates? But the Anglo-Saxon historian describing Alfred's victory speaks of no celebrations until three weeks after Guthrum's acceptance of Alfred's terms, when the Christian king led the pagan Guthrum and thirty of the Viking king's most trusted noblemen to a small church in the village of Aller to receive the sacrament of baptism.

The choice of the seemingly insignificant church at Aller for this ceremony may seem, at first, difficult to explain. One would expect Alfred to choose a church whose size and splendor would impress upon Guthrum the greatness of Alfred's kingdom and the glory of his reign. It would seem to make more sense for Alfred to have conducted this ceremony in the royal city of Winchester, where Alfred could have overwhelmed Guthrum with his own majesty and kingliness. Instead Alfred chose the very humble village church of Aller, a modest church constructed of wood rather than stone, set deep in the remote wilds of Wessex.

Aller sits just a short walk to the east of Athelney, in the midst of the wastelands that had provided Alfred with shelter throughout his desperate winter exile. It was at this meager shack of a church that Alfred had worshiped as a hunted fugitive. For some reason, he felt a strong urge to share the scenery of his banishment with the Viking who had until recently hunted him. Perhaps he wanted to show Guthrum the landscape of his exile, pointing out where he had hidden as the Danish troops scoured the countryside for him. Or perhaps, having spent countless hours in prayer in the ramshackle church of Aller begging God for deliverance from the Viking invasion, now Alfred felt a strong pull to bring Guthrum back to this very church, an acknowledgment that those prayers were being answered in this baptism.

Silently the mixed procession of Wessex noblemen and Viking chieftains wound their way upon the path alongside the river Parrett, leading to the village of Aller. Looming large on the horizon sat Burrow Mump, from whose heights Alfred's men had regularly stood wary watch, ready to send word to the forces hidden at Athelney of approaching Danes. It had been five weeks since the great Saxon victory at Edington, and the wounds of the noblemen had largely healed.

After the parade of warriors arrived at the church of Aller, they were greeted at the door by the priest who was to conduct the ceremony. For Guthrum and his men, the following ceremony must have felt bizarre and foreign. The ninth-century liturgy for baptism was filled with a number of symbolic ceremonies designed to portray the significance of taking on the Christian faith and the necessity of turning from all elements of paganism. But for the priest conducting the ceremony, as well as for the Christian noblemen who stood watching, this baptismal liturgy must have seemed entirely foreign as well. The Anglo-Saxons administered baptism as soon after birth as possible. A family who waited more than thirty days to baptize their newborn child could be subject to a fine. Thus, the spectacle of a crowd of grown men, seasoned warriors, all being escorted into a church in their white robes to receive baptism, must have been an almost humorous sight. It is likely that this was the first time any of the men of Wessex had ever seen a grown man baptized.

In the early church, new converts to Christianity would spend a lengthy period of time as a *catechumen* before receiving baptism. A catechumen was someone who had made an initial commitment to the Christian faith but was still learning the basic elements of Christianity and searching his heart to ensure he was truly prepared to be baptized (which would usually be performed on either Easter or Pentecost). But for the Anglo-Saxons, whose lives were a little more uncertain and the odds of living until the next Easter or Pentecost seemed much slimmer, it was thought that baptism should be administered as soon as possible, so the church dispensed with the intervening months or years that many Christians spent as catechumens preparing for baptism. Therefore, the Anglo-Saxons combined the two ceremonies of being received as a catechumen and of receiving baptism. Becoming a catechumen was performed at the door of the church, and was referred to as the *cristnung*. Now a catechumen, the candidate for baptism was immediately led to the font for baptism.

The *cristnung* began with the *exsufflatio*, in which the priest would blow on the face of the candidate. The blowing was attended with a prayer, which explained that the breath of God would terrify the devil and drive him out, freeing the candidate from the lusts of the flesh. Next, the priest placed a bit of salt under the man's tongue, which by its pungency signified the power of divinely given wisdom. Then the priest wet the recipient's ears and nostrils with his own spittle, to show that wisdom would come to him through hearing and smelling. Last, he anointed him with oil in the shape of the cross on his chest and on his back, to declare that the cross would form a shield for this man to protect him from Satan's fiery darts from in front and from behind. With that, the *cristnung* was complete, and the Danes, now catechumens, proceeded on to the baptismal font.

Here Guthrum was met by King Alfred, who stood next to the Dane as his sponsor while he renounced Satan and professed his new faith in Jesus Christ. At this, the priest plunged the Viking's head into the font, immersing him three times, in the name of the Father, the Son, and the Holy Ghost. And with this last immersion, Alfred, as his sponsor, grasped Guthrum by the shoulders and lifted him up from the water, now a Christian man. By doing so, Alfred received Guthrum from baptism, meaning he took the Dane as his own godson. In addition to his new faith, Guthrum also received a new name at his baptism, a Christian name. He was now called Æthelstan, godson of King Alfred.

By taking Guthrum as his godson, Alfred intended to form a bond of kinship between himself and the conquered Viking ruler, a bond that would hopefully help maintain peace between the Saxons and the Danes. The creation of familial connections between the ruling families of two different kingdoms had been a common way of trying to create a fondness between nations. Alfred's older sister, Æthelswith, had been given in marriage to Burgred, the Mercian king, in an attempt to maintain an alliance with that once great Saxon nation. Alfred's wife, Ealswith, was descended from the Mercian royal family as well, and Alfred's fondness for his wife helped to keep a fondness for Mercia in his heart.

Of course these marriages merely worked to preserve an already healthy alliance between Wessex and Mercia. Other marriages were contracted with the goal of reconciling two estranged or warring kingdoms. When a king's daughter was given to marry into the royal family of an enemy nation, she was considered to be a *frithwebba*, a "peace-weaver." By being taken as a wife into the enemy's family and producing children for her new husband, this woman wove the two warring factions together into one family. This practice of using marriage to secure international peace was used by the Viking nations just as much as by the Saxons. The theory of the custom was intuitively understood by all, though in actuality the practice often failed to bring about any lasting peace.

Alfred's sponsorship of Guthrum at his baptism drew upon the same principle as the *frithwebba*. The Christian church had long understood from Jesus' words to Nicodemus in John 3:5 that the entrance into the Christian faith was a kind of rebirth. Medieval Christians took this imagery seriously and insisted that this second spiritual birth included many of the same elements as the first physical birth. Since one had physical parents at that first birth, then one must also have spiritual parents at this second birth. Therefore, at baptism each candidate was accompanied by a man or woman who sponsored this new Christian as godparent and pledged to act as a spiritual mentor. The relationship of godfather to godson was considered to be every bit as real as the relationship between father and son. For instance, not long after Alfred's time, it was considered a violation of biblical law if a man were to marry his goddaughter, since the marriage of a father to his daughter would be considered incestuous. To act as godfather at an Anglo-Saxon baptism was to invite the baptized man into one's family.

By acting as Guthrum's godfather, Alfred essentially adopted the conquered and converted the Dane, becoming his spiritual father. In doing so, Alfred sought to weave a true and lasting peace between the nation of Wessex and the invading Danes, bringing them into his church and into his home.

After Guthrum, now Æthelstan, godson of King Alfred, had been baptized, the sign of the cross was marked upon his forehead with oil, confirming his baptism, and his head was bound with a white cloth. All the men receiving baptism were then robed entirely in white, symbolizing that the rags of their old lives had been removed and they were now united with the risen Christ through this second birth and were clothed with his glory. All the newly baptized Vikings were to wear these robes for the next week. Immediately after the service, Alfred led the host of new Christians to his royal estate in the village of Wedmore, one day's journey to the north of Aller.

At Wedmore, Alfred treated his godson, along with Guthrum's thirty Danish companions, to twelve days of Anglo-Saxon feasting. The Viking guests, once the mortal enemies of the Wessex throne, now sat in Alfred's raucous mead hall, white-robed, banqueting on roasted boar and venison, draining horns of mead, and listening to the Saxon scop thrumming on his lyre and singing poems of the glory of long-dead warriors, mingled with lyrics praising the most high God who had created the wonder-filled world.

Each of these twelve days of feasting was filled with festivities and entertainment—hunting, horse races, foot races, archery, wrestling, and all the sports that delighted the Saxons most. The nights were filled with feasting and the music of the scop. Then, well into the feasting, each night Alfred would open up his treasure hoard and begin to bestow on his guests mountains of splendid gifts. His largesse flowed unrestrained by any resentment of the previous years of hostility between himself and his guests. Rather than vengeance, Alfred offered forgiveness, a forgiveness made clear through the great Saxon virtue of gift giving. Pattern-welded swords with their serpentine-etched blades, magnificent helms crested with fierce boars, gilded and jewelled, finely crafted brooches and pendants—all these and more were handed over to the Viking guests.

But most important of all, King Alfred gave his guests rings, the gift that most conveyed the relationship that Alfred had established with Guthrum. King Alfred was once again the ring-giver of Wessex, sitting enthroned in the mead hall, with his faithful thegns surrounding him, eating his meat, drinking his mead, taking his gifts, and pledging their allegiance to him. And here Guthrum sat, now a Christian named Æthelstan, receiving Alfred's gifts and pledging faithfulness to the king of Wessex.

On the eighth day, the Viking guests celebrated the *crismlysing*, that is, the removal of the white robes and chrism (the white cloth that had been bound over their foreheads, where they had been anointed after their baptism). The chrism of Æthelstan was removed by Æthelnoth, the ealdorman of Somerset. Æthelnoth had been one of Alfred's most faithful companions throughout his exile and had worked closely with the king during his hiding at Athelney in Somerset. By removing Æthelstan's chrism, Æthelnoth essentially became a second godfather to the baptized Viking, since sponsorship at the crismlysing was considered equivalent to sponsorship at baptism.

After the crismlysing, the festivities continued another four days. At the end of the feasting and gift giving, the two kings went their separate ways. Alfred returned to Winchester, his capital city, to begin rebuilding his nation. Æthelstan returned to what remained of his army, still barricaded within the makeshift fortress of Chippenham. Alfred allowed Æthelstan to stay for several more months at Chippenham, giving him time to arrange for his next move. By October the Viking forces had left Wessex altogether and had marched north, to Cirencester in Mercia, on the northern border of Wessex. Mercia had been ruled by Ceolwulf, the puppet king whom Halfdan and Guthrum had left in charge when the Mercian king Burgred had fled to Rome. Now it was Ceolwulf's turn to realize that his presence was no longer necessary. Soon, Ceolwulf had been moved along, and Mercia was ruled by Æthelstan alone.

In one sense, it would seem that Alfred had been thoroughly victorious in his struggle. He had triumphed in a battle that had seemed only a few months before to be utterly hopeless. Not only had he conquered his enemy, but he had conquered his enemy by converting his foe into a friend. But Alfred was not so gullible as to think that just because Guthrum had been conquered once, he would then submit ever and always to Alfred's commands. Alfred knew his Viking opponent well enough to know that a Dane could say whatever was necessary to win peace and then, a moment later, betray all his promises and strike out once more. And although Alfred firmly believed that baptism into the Father, Son, and Holy Ghost worked a powerful mystery on all those who received that sacrament, he also knew that the wickedness of the human heart was fully capable of twisting even that great sacrament into a deceitful weapon, used to beguile the credulous Christian into an easily exploited complacency.

Alfred still hoped that a lasting change had been worked on Æthelstan, though he watched his new godson closely with a sceptical eye. Alfred's hopes turned to deep concern when Æthelstan's army, still camped on the northern border of Wessex, was joined several months later by a new Viking army, recently arrived from plundering on the continent and now camped on the Mercian northern bank of the Thames at Fulham, just past London. Was this newly arrived army of fresh Viking troops a reinforcement for one more attack on Wessex? Would Æthelstan's renouncing of his former life at the church of Aller prove to be only a temporary repentance? Had Æthelstan reverted to Guthrum?

CHAPTER 6

Rebuilding Wessex

And I said to them, "You see the trouble that we are in,
how Jerusalem lies desolate and her gates have burned
with fire. Come, let us build the wall of Jerusalem, so
that we are no longer a reproach."

—NEHEMIAH 2:17

G uthrum's sudden conversion to the
Christianity of the Anglo-Saxons and
the taking of the Saxon name Æthelstan
may have been difficult to believe. Was the Viking
king's sudden embracing of the Christian faith a
genuine and heartfelt repentance of his pagan past?
Or was it a pragmatic decision, cunningly chosen
to exploit the weakness and gullibility of Alfred's
faith? The scholarly method tends to veer toward the
more cynical interpretation, presupposing that only
the basest motivations lay behind every decision:

Guthrum must have received baptism because it bought him time to remove his troops peacefully, only to strike again at a later date. Or possibly, Guthrum had resigned himself to the fact that Alfred would remain in control of Wessex, and the conquered Viking saw that as a godson to the only reigning Saxon king he would be woven into the web of Saxon nobles and given opportunities to increase his own power and wealth.

Jesus described in a parable the problem of the short-lived conversion, likening the temporary convert to seed thrown onto rocky soil where its roots could not grow deep (Matthew 13:3–9). The seed sprouts at first, but with such shallow roots and impeded by the rocky soil, it is unable to endure the heat of the afternoon sun and quickly withers and shrivels away. Other seed is eaten up immediately by the birds or choked to death by crowding thorns. But some seed falls on good soil and endures throughout the growing season, bringing in a bountiful harvest.

The true convert, Jesus later explained, was like this enduring seed. His faith persevered to the end of his fruitful life. So what kind of seed was Æthelstan? Was this new faith to be quickly choked out by the cares of the world? Would it lack perseverance? Or would his profession of faith endure to the end? With great concern, Alfred waited for the answer to this question.

The arrival of a fresh band of plunder-eager Vikings provided the first test of Æthelstan's sincerity. In the late autumn of 878, this new Danish army camped at Fullham, on the northern bank of the

Thames, just west of London. Then, having settled in for the winter, the Fullham Vikings sent word to Æthelstan in Cirencester, seeking to form a mutually profitable alliance with the Viking by which they might plunder the kingdom of Wessex.

In Winchester, Alfred received regular messages from his thegns about the movements of this new band of Vikings and of Æthelstan, who was still camped at Cirencester, perched menacingly on Alfred's northern border. From the intelligence he was able to gather, it seemed likely he would soon be facing his godson in battle once more, reinforced with a fresh supply of Danish warriors. Then, doubling his suspicions, one afternoon shortly after the Vikings made their camp on the bank of the Thames, all of Wessex fell under a shadow of terrible darkness as a shield as black as death slowly swallowed the sun and all its brightness and heat.

This solar eclipse was reported by a number of contemporary Anglo-Saxon historians. And though it was understood by Alfred and all the thegns of his court that the eclipse of the sun was always a significant portent, it was unclear just how this particular omen should be interpreted. Did it signal the apostasy of Æthelstan and one more devastating Danish assault on the nation of Wessex? Or was it a confirmation that Alfred's victory at Edington had made his rule over Wessex sure and unequivocal?

The answer to these questions was soon made clear. Æthelstan refused the invitation from the Vikings at Fullham and sent their emissaries away from his court empty-handed. The Vikings of Fullham, seeing there was no chance of an alliance with Æthelstan and realizing the resolve of Alfred and his battle-hardened men, abandoned their hopes for easy Saxon plunder and at the end of

winter climbed back into their ships to sail for the European continent where resistance to plundering bands was less resolute.

Sailing away in 879, these Vikings established a base in Ghent
and spent the next several years slaughtering and plundering the
surrounding monasteries and convents. Æthelstan, however, stayed
true to the vows of his baptism and pulled his own troops away from
the northern border of Wessex, leaving Cirencester to march back to
East Anglia, where he settled into life as a Christian king, ruling over
the people of East Anglia.

Though it may be difficult to be entirely rid of suspicions about
the sincerity of Æthelstan's faith, the evidence indicates that Æthelstan
was the good seed, fallen on fertile soil and yielding a bountiful
harvest. He refused to join the Viking raiders in their planned attack
on Wessex, and throughout the years, he maintained the peace
between himself and Alfred, entering into several treaties with the
Wessex king. After his baptism, he never gave reason to believe that
he was anything other than a sincere Christian.

When the East Anglian king later minted his own coinage, it
was his Christian name—Æthelstan—that appeared on every coin,
rather than his former Viking name, Guthrum. During the following
decades, however, the coin to become the most popular coin in all
of Danish East Anglia was the Saint Edmund penny, a silver coin
that had been minted to commemorate the martyrdom of Edmund,
the Christian king of East Anglia who had been struck down by the
pagan chieftains Ubbe and Ivar, Guthrum's former comrades. What a
tremendous irony that within two decades of Edmund's martyrdom,
his murderers would be converted to his faith and would begin issu-
ing commemorative coins to remember his death.

Ten years later, when King Æthelstan died, the *Anglo-Saxon Chronicle* recorded his death and described him as the northern king, whose baptismal name was Æthelstan, the godson of Alfred. No mention was made of his life as a Viking or his years of waging war against Wessex. He was simply Alfred's godson.

The departure of the Viking force that had been encamped at Fullham, together with the new alliance formed with Æthelstan, left Alfred and his weary kingdom with an unexpected respite from military campaigns. Alfred understood that this peace would only be temporary, since other Northmen seeking plunder would inevitably come to try their luck at despoiling the wealth of Wessex. Therefore, this respite from the Viking-inflicted bloodshed could not be spent in peaceful rest and relaxation, feasting and drinking in the mead hall, and enjoying the intensely refreshing English summer. Rather, this was a surprising lull in the storm that offered a brief, but much needed, chance to rethink the organization of the defenses of Wessex and to better prepare the Saxon military for fighting off future invasions. If Alfred was to hold together the last Anglo-Saxon nation against future Viking onslaughts, then the Wessex military needed to be restructured to better respond to the Danish threat, and this moment of peace offered the king of Wessex time to accomplish just that.

The necessary military reforms required Alfred to give some thought to the strengths of the Viking armies and how they had managed to exploit the weaknesses of the defenses of Wessex. It was now clear that the real strength of the Vikings was not necessarily their ferocity in battle. The Wessex army had regularly been able to hold their shieldwall while facing down their Viking enemies. The problem the Saxons repeatedly encountered was the swiftness and cunning of the Viking armies.

Between the inexhaustible network of rivers criss-crossing the British countryside—which the Danes were able to exploit with their shallow draft boats and expert seamanship—and the still-functional Roman road system that afforded great mobility to mounted Danish troops, the Vikings were able to move at a speed that no Saxon fyrd could match. They struck and plundered the easily gained wealth of undefended towns and then moved on long before any military aid could be sent to defend the victims of the raid. Then, on the rare occasions when the Saxon fyrds were able to respond quickly enough to actually corner the Viking raiders, the Danes merely fortified whatever town had last fallen victim to them and waited for the Saxons to tire of the siege and resign themselves to paying the danegeld.

If Wessex was to resist future Viking assaults, then it was imperative that Alfred construct a defensive system capable of countering the incredibly swift mobility of the Viking troops, a system that would rob the Danes of the ability to wait out a protracted siege only to be rewarded with a payment of danegeld.

The king had always maintained a small force of professional soldiers attached to his court who were capable of responding quickly to military threats. These were the men who dwelt in Alfred's hall, drinking his mead and pledging him their blades. They were a stouthearted troop—faithful, intrepid, and sword-savvy. But this force of loyal thegns numbered less than two hundred men and thus was far too small to face the larger raiding armies of more than one thousand Northmen, which had begun to plague England during Alfred's reign.

The larger voluntary shire fyrds, which formed the bulk of Wessex's military might, were drawn from the landowning noblemen and other freemen of Wessex. They could be a fierce force when they stood defending the farms, homesteads, and villages of their native land, but they could be painfully slow to mobilize, often requiring weeks to wrap up their obligations at home and finally prepare themselves for battle. When they were finally mobilized, the work that had been left undone on the farms and in the shops back at home, as well as the families that had been left unguarded, weighed heavily on their minds. Thus their loyalty to the ongoing military campaign would frequently begin to wane when the campaign dragged on indefinitely during the siege of a Viking fortification and kept them from fulfilling their duties at home.

Rectifying this problem would require that Alfred effect a massive reform of the Wessex military. To quickly field an army large enough to fend off the Viking armies, Alfred could no longer rely on the sluggish response of the traditional fyrd. Instead, he would need to maintain a large standing army of soldiers skilled in war craft who were ready to respond to an invading army at a moment's notice.

Alfred divided the entire Wessex fyrd into halves and insisted that each half take turns mobilizing and preparing for combat. This left each town with half of their combat-eligible noblemen and freemen overseeing the work in the fields and other necessary chores, while the other half provided the necessary military service, waiting battle-ready to respond to any possible Viking attacks. Although this put a heavy strain on the local economies by permanently absenting half of the landowners, it guaranteed that, even in moments of national emergency, no more than half of the leading men would be called away for fyrd service. Since the rotation between working at home and standing ready in the fyrd was scheduled and predictable, the disruption of the work schedule was much more easily mitigated.

The men in this new standing army were divided into two sections. One portion became a highly mobile army, camped in the fields of Wessex and waiting for news of any possible threat to the Saxon peace. The men of this army were required to provide their own horses, as well as enough food for sixty days, giving this large army the ability to travel the length of the nation in several days and to wage war at a moment's notice. The other portion of the standing army was assigned to guard a collection of fortified cities and towns spaced evenly across the breadth of Wessex. This division of the military provided Alfred with a highly mobile offensive force, which could travel quickly to confront any intruding threat, as well as a defensive garrison guarding each of the fortified cities. Thus Alfred ensured that no matter where he moved his mobile force, the cities of Wessex were protected.

By keeping a defensive force in these cities, Alfred robbed wandering Viking armies of the ability to easily seize an unprotected city and fortify it against the Saxon army. Additionally, the knowledge that there was another army guarding the families and farms left behind gave peace of mind to the soldiers serving in the mobile army and the ability to more resolutely pursue their enemies far and wide. And, since the military also acted as the Anglo-Saxon "police force," the presence of an organized force throughout the nation significantly improved the law and order of the cities, towns, and villages of Wessex.

Alfred's innovations in organizing the garrisons that would defend the fortified cities of Wessex constitute probably the greatest administrative accomplishment of his reign. First, the king carefully selected thirty Wessex cities to receive garrison forces from the rotating fyrd. Each of these cities was positioned within around twenty miles (or one day's march) of one another, forming a network of fortified cities that covered the extent of Wessex.

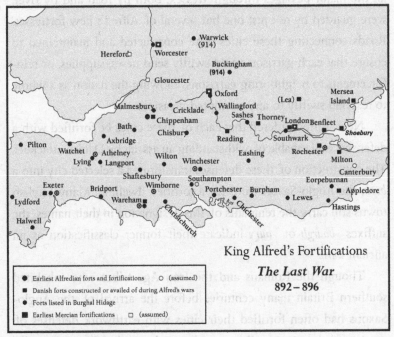

King Alfred's Fortifications

The Last War

892–896

- ● Earliest Alfredian forts and fortifications   ○ (assumed)
- ■ Danish forts constructed or availed of during Alfred's wars
- ● Forts listed in Burghal Hidage
- ■ Earliest Mercian fortifications   □ (assumed)

© MARK ROSS/SURFACEWORKS

Some of these cities, such as Bath, Chichester, Hastings, and Winchester, had long histories that reached back to the Roman occupation of Britain. The unusually regular grids of the ancient streets provided a helpful footing upon which Alfred built, exploiting the firm foundations the Roman ruins offered as well as maintaining the efficiency of the older city layouts. Some cities, like Cissanbyrig, Brydian, and Halwell, were built on the ancient Iron Age hill-forts taking advantage of the defenses offered by their lofty heights and still-standing earthwork walls. Other city-fortresses were built as entirely new constructions, where no significant settlement had previously stood. Each city's location was carefully chosen to ensure that all the major passages through Wessex, both by road and by river, were guarded by not just one but several of Alfred's new fortresses. Roads connecting these cities were constructed and maintained to ensure that each garrison could swiftly send news, supplies, or reinforcements to neighboring garrisons, allowing the nation as a whole to respond swiftly to any attempted invasion.

Next, Alfred ordered that each of these cities be fortified with a defensive wall capable of withstanding an assault by Danish attackers. The construction of these defenses transformed a selected city into a *burh*, the Anglo-Saxon word for a fortified dwelling. Many English towns still carry the remnants of this designation in their names; the suffixes *-bourgh* or *-bury* indicate their former classification as an ancient *burh*.

Though the Romans and the Iron Age tribes who inhabited southern Britain many centuries before the arrival of the Anglo-Saxons had often fortified their cities with earthwork defenses of moats and dykes, as well as wooden and occasionally stone walls, the defenses erected in Wessex during Alfred's reign were the first defensive fortifications built in Wessex throughout the Anglo-Saxon era. A deep moat and a newly constructed wall encircling the city defended each of the thirty burhs.

Where possible, the Saxons used ancient Roman or Iron Age moats and walls, rebuilding the ancient stone walls and deepening the defensive ditches. But many of the new burhs lacked any pre-existing fortifications and required that the entire ditch and wall structure be built fresh. In these cases, the Saxons opted primarily for the swifter method of building with wood, rather than stone. The burh walls included a fighting platform circling the inside of the palisade, from which the defenders could fire arrows or even stones on an attacking force. Many of the walls were also equipped with defensive towers and gatehouses.

After the walls were constructed, Alfred devised a unique method of calculating the troops to be stationed within each burh at any given time. The wall of each burh was measured in "poles," an Anglo-Saxon unit of length that corresponded to approximately five and a half yards. One pole of fortified wall required four men to properly defend it. Each of these men represented one "hide" of the surrounding farmland. A hide covered approximately 120 acres. Thus, it was considered reasonable to expect that 120 acres' worth of farmland, or one Anglo-Saxon hide, could supply one man, suited for combat, to defend the fortified walls of the burh. This created a convenient formula for coordinating the size of a burh's wall with the number of men expected to defend that wall, as well as the amount of surrounding farmland necessary to support such a force.

A manuscript dating from shortly after Alfred's reign, known as the *Burghal Hideage*, preserves the total hides prescribed for each of the Wessex burhs. As many of the old city walls of Alfred's burhs have been discovered and measured out, it is shocking how closely these measurements, when run through the formula described above, correspond to the number of hides assigned in the *Burghal Hideage*. For instance, the Saxon walls of Alfred's capital city, Winchester, have been measured recently at 3,318 yards. The *Burghal Hideage* assigned 2,400 hides to the city, requiring that the city wall be defended by the same number of soldiers. At four men per pole, this suggests a total wall length of 600 poles. If each pole stood for 5.5 yards, then the walled perimeter would need to measure a total of 3,300 yards. When compared to the 3,318-yard measurement calculated by modern archaeologists, the numbers listed in the *Burghal Hideage* are remarkably close.

The much smaller burh of Porchester offers a similar testimony. The archaeological evidence suggests a measurement of 697 yards for the original perimeter of the ancient walls. The *Burghal Hideage* assigned 500 hides to Portchester, or 500 men for the burh's defenses. These men could guard 125 poles of city wall, or 687.5 yards.

Alfred set about reworking the network of roads and public places inside the walls with an eye toward ensuring that the burhs would be well prepared to respond swiftly and efficiently to the unpredictable attacks of a besieging army. The king took his inspiration for these new city plans from the pattern used by ancient Roman camps, a pattern still apparent in the road layout of many of the Saxon cities with a Roman history.

Each burh was equipped with one wide street that ran across the diameter of the city, the "high" street, which allowed for the quick movement of troops from one side of the city to the other in order to respond swiftly to the changing tactics of the attacking army. Smaller streets were constructed running parallel or at right angles to the high street, offering quick access to each segment of the wall. Another street was built along the perimeter of the city wall.

This network of roads ensured that a commander could quickly reposition his troops along the city wall to maintain a wall that was properly fortified at all the key points. And though Alfred's thoughts were all of gory battles and bitter sieges when he conceived this layout, the efficiency of his new system became more evident in the mundane daily tasks than it did in any particular combat engagement. It was in the everyday routine of gathering at the carefully planned marketplace or in the weekly habit of walking to Sunday morning worship in the burh minster, that the sensible road pattern became evident. Alfred's layouts are still used in numerous cities, testifying to the efficiency of his plans.

Much like Alfred's new street layouts, the system of defensive burhs, described in the *Burghal Hideage*, was first conceived as a military innovation. But after it had been implemented, it was discovered that this new system radically improved the efficiency with which the king could administrate his kingdom. The network of burhs and the roads that connected them provided travelers and traders the ability to move across Wessex, stopping every night at a walled and garrisoned burh where peace and safety could be guaranteed.

With the safety afforded by the defenses of the burhs, the surrounding areas naturally gravitated toward bringing their produce and wares to the well-protected and well-governed markets. In later generations, kings of Wessex required that all trade occur within one of the designated burh markets, where the king's reeves could ensure that proper taxes were paid to the crown on all sales. An alternative Anglo-Saxon word for burh was *tun*, a term that also referred to a fortified or walled settlement. To this day, an English town, or tun, must feature a town marketplace in order to qualify as a "town." Without this marketplace, it can only be considered a "village." (After a town has a cathedral, it has earned the distinction of "city.")

Under Alfred and the protection that the *Burghal Hideage* ensured, trade and industry began to thrive in Wessex. Seeing the importance of this element of the economy, Alfred also undertook a major renovation of the Saxon currency. When he came to power, only two mints could be found in the nations of the Saxons, one in London and the other in Canterbury. And these two mints produced an extremely crude coin, boasting a severely debased silver content of 20 percent. A thriving industry of trade would require that these deficiencies be fixed. Soon Alfred was giving his attention to these problems.

By the time of Alfred's death, the number of mints under the control of the Wessex crown had more than quadrupled. The new silver pennies that Alfred had ordered to be produced were almost pure silver and, even with this much higher degree of purity, still significantly outweighed the previous coinage. In order to mint these new silver pennies, four of the earlier pennies needed to be melted down to provide enough silver for one new penny. The cost was substantial, but the king believed that a restored confidence in the currency would attract the attention of Europe's traders and eventually would bring a much greater amount of wealth to the nation.

In addition to this penny, Alfred also introduced the half-penny to the English currency. This smaller coin gave merchants the ability to more conveniently sell smaller items. Altogether, Alfred's innovations had a tremendous impact on the economy of Wessex, catching the attention of merchants throughout Europe who were drawn to the wealth of the newly thriving English nation.

Although the years following Alfred's victory over Guthrum were characterized by peace within the borders of Wessex, this was only relative to the earlier years of constant Viking occupation. Alfred still had to contend with regular raiding parties of freebooting Danes striking quickly along the coasts and rivers of the Anglo-Saxons, searching for easy plunder. In the year 882, the king received word of one such fleet of Vikings sailing off the coast of Wessex, hunting for easy spoils. Alfred moved quickly to intercept the Viking naval force and engage the invading pirates in ship-to-ship combat.

The Saxon sailors, led by Alfred, still fighting like a wild boar, overtook four Danish boats. They boarded the Viking vessels and set to work with axe and sword, hewing and slashing their way through the Danish fleet. The crews of the first two Viking ships were entirely slaughtered within minutes. Then, as the bloodied but still battle-hungry Saxons spilled into the hull of the next ship, cutting their way on board, the Vikings quickly lost their stomach for the fight. They surrendered and begged for mercy from Alfred, as the historian records, "on bended knee."

It is interesting that several years after wresting his great victory from Guthrum and establishing peace throughout Wessex, Alfred could still be found personally commanding these smaller combat missions. Though the king was not present for each and every military engagement fought by the Wessex troops, Alfred, until his death, regularly took his sword, shield, and spear into battle, standing shoulder to shoulder in the shieldwall with his countrymen. In the Anglo-Saxon world, combat was the duty of the ruling class; and the king, his thegns, the noblemen, and other rulers of the English people always filled the ranks of the Wessex shieldwall.

Thus, it was the landed class, not the peasants or slaves, who responded to the summons of the fyrd and were expected to die on the battlefield. Though this system may have had its faults, when compared to modern societies where liberty has made great advances against this class system, there remains something about the Anglo-Saxon mentality that was nobler than the governing practices of modern nations. In Alfred's day, no man could order another into combat to face a gory death in battle if he wasn't prepared to stand next to him in that same perilous fight. The image of a king ordering his troops to battle while he sat luxuriously pavilioned far from the place of slaughter was the innovation of a much later age and inconceivable to the Anglo-Saxon mind.

In the year 885, Alfred's many innovations for the defenses of his territories were put to the test. The Danish army, who had earlier camped at Fullham near London and had tested the sincerity of Æthelstan's baptismal vows, suddenly returned to Wessex hoping to find that several years of peace from Viking raids would have caused the Anglo-Saxons to grow complacent, lax, and vulnerable. This particular raiding army had spent the intervening seven years between their departure from England and their sudden return pillaging the abbeys, priories, and monasteries of northern Europe.

Alfred had actually carefully followed their gruesome career throughout the Franks' river systems and knew full well of their bloody attack on the ancient monastery of Saint Bertin in West Francia; their progress into Flanders where they forced the people of Ghent to shelter them through the winter; their seizing of horses for their entire force, making their raiding army a mounted troop; their ravaging up the river Oise to Rheims; their attack on the convent of Condé, where the nuns were forced at sword point to provide for their Viking guests for an entire year; their slaughter up and down the rivers Lys, Scheldt, Meuse, Rhine, Moselle, and finally the Somme. And Alfred heard how this particular force had been rewarded for their theft and murder with repeated payments of the danegeld by the Christian rulers in Europe, men like Charles the Fat and Carloman. Then, in the early winter months of 885, Alfred received the ominous message that this army had divided its forces into two, one half choosing to push deeper into East Francia, while the other half returned to England expecting to be rewarded with a tremendous harvest of plunder in those fields that had been left fallow for so long.

By the time the Britain-bound portion of the Viking fleet landed on the shores of Kent, the English winter was well under way. For the last several years, the Danish policy had been to choose a strategic wintering point, a well-provisioned and poorly defended site, which could be overthrown quickly, held throughout the winter, drained of its wealth and stores, and then abandoned in spring as the river waters surged and other potential victims beckoned.

Their arrival on the shores of England late into the season put the Danes significantly behind schedule, so they wasted little time in selecting their target and striking swiftly. The Viking army chose the city of Rochester, a former Roman settlement sitting on the banks of the river Medway a short distance from the river mouth, where the waters mingle with the Thames in the Thames estuary before flowing into the North Sea.

At the beginning of the seventh century, Rochester had been converted to the Christian faith by the missionary Justus, who had been sent to the city by the newly arrived Augustine of Canterbury. As a result of Justus's efforts, England's second oldest cathedral was soon built in Rochester, bringing to the ancient city, over the following centuries, all the wealth such an eminent cathedral might attract. This meant that the city of Rochester was blessed with two of the Vikings' favorite features—a navigable river and a wealthy church.

Although the city of Rochester sat in Kent and was therefore not included in Alfred's plans for the reconstruction of the defenses of Wessex, the subkingdoms Alfred ruled—Kent, Essex, and Sussex— had all undergone similar programs of reform. Thus the city walls of Rochester had been quite recently refortified to ensure they were constructed to provide the same sort of protection offered in any of the burhs of Wessex. Additionally, the nobles and landowners had organized a garrisoned fighting force equivalent to the stipulations of the *Burghal Hideage*, a force sufficient to ensure that the newly constructed walls were well defended. For the Vikings, the strength of Rochester would prove to be astonishing.

It would seem that the time elapsed from the moment the dreaded Viking longboats came into view, their dragon-carved prows slicing through the foamy waters of the Thames estuary and then turning to sail up the mouth of the Medway, until the pillaging Danes spilled out of their ships to charge the city would have left little time for a warning to have traveled through enough of the surrounding region to gather any sort of significant fighting force within the city walls.

And so when the Viking horde charged the gates of Rochester splitting the air with their gore-hungry screams, they fully expected to spend little more than a moment hewing through the city's defenses, leaving the rest of their afternoon free for despoiling the city and the surrounding countryside. That the gates had been bolted against them was not a great surprise to the attacking Danes. But when they drew near the walls to begin smashing down the massive city doors, they were astonished to discover that the many fighting platforms situated along the towering city walls were manned by a substantial contingent of battle-ready Kentish men who eagerly greeted the startled Vikings with a shower of arrows, spears, and rocks.

The initial chaos of the desperate flight from the walls of Rochester, accompanied by the terrifying chorus of shrieks and howls of those who had fallen in the artillery-inflicted carnage, suggested for a brief moment that the Viking force would fall into a total and easily conquered pandemonium. But the disciplined and battle-savvy Danes quickly regained their composure and regrouped just beyond the range of the Kentish archery.

The Viking chieftains were resilient and able to reassess a situation and quickly change their tactics to suit the ever-shifting challenges they faced on the battlefield. Seeing that a direct assault on the walls of Rochester was likely to cost the lives of a great number of Vikings, the Danes resigned themselves to a prolonged siege. Confident in their ability to outlast whatever provisions the men of Kent had hoarded within the city walls, the Danes settled in to wait until the hunger pains of Rochester drove the men to accept the terms of the Northmen—to pay the danegeld.

Having been startled once by the Saxon's strength, however, the Northmen decided to ensure that their siege was conducted from the safety of a properly fortified position. Soon the Danes began digging a circle of ditch and dike earthwork defenses, constructing a carefully barricaded camp just beyond the gates of Rochester. As the excavation began, another contingent of the Vikings searched out the nearest pastures to find forage for the multitude of horses the Viking troops had brought with them from Normandy in the hopes of using their mounts to wander far and wide from the Kentish river systems. During the following days, the Danes mounted a series of attacks against the defenses of Rochester in the hopes of finding some weakness in the Kentish fortress, some chink in the Saxon armor. But they found none and were driven back from Rochester's walls on every occasion. Still it seemed that it would only be a matter of time before the besieged city's determination flagged and the danegeld would ultimately be surrendered.

Although the Viking commanders expected that a shire fyrd would eventually be mustered to contend with them, it was assumed that the gathering of the fyrd would take some time and that by the time the Saxon army arrived, the earthwork fortress would provide more than enough protection to the Danish army. Whatever help

Rochester might receive, the Vikings were confident that the siege of the city would continue regardless.

To the stupefying horror of the Vikings, however, only a few days after the raiding army beached its longboats on the banks of the Medway, they received word that an enormous throng of Saxon soldiers was swiftly approaching on horseback. Hardly had the message been brought to the ears of the Viking commanders than the approaching army crested the horizon, innumerable and riding hard, rushing to relieve the besieged city. Not only was this army much larger than expected (being the newly formed standing army of Wessex, rather than the traditional ad hoc shire fyrd), but the ranks of this new force were filled with Saxon men who had spent months training and preparing specifically for a battle such as this. Resolute and battle-hungry, the Wessex forces galloped, with the king of Wessex himself, King Alfred, riding in the vanguard.

The Northmen were thunderstruck. Their typical cool-headed composure evaporated, and they were overwhelmed by a desperate terror and a desire to be as far away from the Anglo-Saxon army as possible. The idea of forming a shieldwall to face Alfred was unthinkable. But the chance of successfully defending the only partially constructed earthwork fortification was equally hopeless. The only attractive option to any of the Viking minds was a dash for safety. The fortress was abandoned. The horses brought across the sea from Europe were left behind. The many Flemish, Frankish, and Anglo-Saxon captives, whom the Vikings had been collecting with the plans of placing them on the lucrative slave market, were all abandoned. In an instant, everything was left behind in one desperate sprint to the Viking longboats.

In the bedlam of the hasty retreat, the Danish army was divided in half. One half managed to reach the beached ships ahead of the advancing Saxons and was able to sail safely down the Medway into the Thames estuary; and without even looking back, they crossed the channel and returned to Europe. The remaining troop of Vikings, overtaken by the cavalry of Wessex, threw themselves on Alfred's mercy, hoping the king would be willing to offer them some terms of peace.

Fortunately for this band of stranded Danes, the king was prepared to be compassionate and allowed them to leave in peace, having taken a selection of Viking hostages and received their vows never again to plunder within Alfred's borders. Perhaps it was a disappointment for the Wessex army to have trained intensely for years and ridden hard for several days only to have the Danes flee the moment the Wessex army approached. But clearly there was good reason to consider the episode a victory for the Anglo-Saxons. Rochester was liberated. The slaves and horses held by the Danes had been abandoned to the Saxons. The Vikings had fled without receiving one piece of danegeld.

There was also good reason to be unsatisfied with the outcome of this encounter. Predictably, the terms of peace the Vikings had used to purchase their freedom were quickly broken as the army again plundered south of the Thames, within Alfred's land. Even more disconcerting, this raiding band seemed to be working in conjunction with another Danish force based in East Anglia. Though King Æthelstan had proved faithful to his vows and never again raided in Wessex, not all of the noblemen under the converted Viking were as prepared to honor the terms of Æthelstan's peace with Alfred. Wanting to send a picture of the power of Wessex to the East Anglian kingdom, Alfred ordered the English navy, loaded with the fighting men of Kent, to move north up the coastline of Kent seeking out opportunities to challenge the Viking fleets.

Upon reaching the mouth of the river Stour, the Wessex fleet immediately encountered a line of sixteen Danish longboats, fully rigged for battle. Immediately the Vikings advanced to meet the Saxons, and a vicious sea battle commenced. Assuming the Viking vessels were manned by an average of thirty men per ship, the Danish force likely had nearly five hundred men in the engagement. It is not known exactly how many fighting men the Wessex navy brought, but it is likely that the English force significantly outnumbered the Danes. Hours of fierce ship-to-ship combat followed, punctuated by occasional intense chases as one ship broke free of the flotilla and rowed madly for safety only to be overtaken, boarded, and forced back into the fight; finally the slaughter ended with every single Viking boat captured, her crews dispatched, and her plunder seized.

Exulting in the triumph and heavy-laden with their pillaged winnings, the Wessex navy finally regrouped and turned to move back down the Stour, anxious to return home and begin the celebrations. However, from the moment the naval combat had begun, word of the arrival of the Wessex fleet and her bold attack on the Danes had been passed to every Viking crew in the vicinity. By the time the Anglo-Saxons had hoisted their sails to begin a leisurely journey home, an enormous Danish fleet had gathered to meet the Saxon navy at the mouth of the Stour and exact their revenge. This time it was the Saxons who were outnumbered as the swelling tidal waters of the Stour teemed with Viking longboats, swarming the battle-weary Saxon fleet. The battle ended poorly for the Saxons that day as all was lost to the victorious Viking navy.

This series of engagements provided Alfred with several important lessons. First, the theory behind his massive reorganization of the Wessex defenses was perfectly sound. A network of well-fortified burhs, combined with a swiftly moving standing army had the potential to completely immunize Wessex from the tactics of the Danish raiding armies that had so plagued the Anglo-Saxons. But the second lesson proved more discouraging. The Danes still ruled the sea. Until Wessex could rob the Vikings of this strength, until Alfred could successfully defend his own shorelines, England would never truly be free from the plague of the Northmen.

The thought that the Danes still dominated the coasts of Britain weighed heavily on Alfred's mind, and he often turned his mind to the problem of his navy, wondering how the Saxons could possibly find an advantage over the navies of the Danes. Alfred, however, was not interested in finding the solution to this problem purely out of a concern for the coasts of Britain. In truth, the king had always been transfixed by the sea and eagerly sought opportunities to sail. Had the obligations of the crown not demanded that he devote his life to the land of Wessex, Alfred would very likely have earned a reputation as an explorer on the sea, the "path of the daring." Alfred's writings regularly employed nautical images and metaphors that hint at the spell the sea had cast on Alfred's mind. Thus, thinking through the renovation of his navy was in many ways an entertaining hobby more than a kingly duty.

It would not be until many years later that Alfred would finally have the opportunity to act upon some of the innovations he had concocted in his daydreams about the Saxon ships. Toward the end of his reign in the year 896, Alfred finally had the opportunity to give his full attention to the Wessex navy and ordered the construction of a fleet of Saxon ships according to a new set of specifications. With an eye toward combating the deadly longboats, having felt the power of these lethal ships skillfully constructed of ash wood, Alfred insisted that the new Saxon boats be almost doubled in size, with sixty oars per ship.

This new design placed more men at the oar, with the hopes of increasing speed in close chases, but more important it ensured that the English boats would arrive for combat with twice the number of soldiers ready for battle. Boarding one of Alfred's longboats would be a much more formidable task. Contemporary accounts of Alfred's new vessels state that the new ships sailed faster, handled better, and rode higher in the water than any other naval design (a tremendous advantage in ship-to-ship fighting). To train his new navy, Alfred recruited a number of experienced Frisian sailors from the continent, men well reputed for their seamanship.

Alfred's foray into shipbuilding and his organization of a standing naval force won for him the title "the Father of England's navy." Predictably, this designation is hotly contested by military historians since it is impossible to trace an unbroken line of descent from Alfred's organization of the Wessex naval forces all the way down to the United Kingdom's present Royal Navy. That position is more likely held by Henry VIII. Thus, the concern to "demythologize" Alfred the Great compels some to object to this title being given to the king of Wessex. But it seems that King Alfred played enough of a prominent role in the origins of the English naval forces that he could reasonably claim some portion of this honorary title.

Alfred's shipbuilding innovations have been the focus of a great deal of scholarly scorn because of a skirmish between Saxon and Danish forces that was fought shortly after the new fleet was constructed. In the year 896, Danish longboats struck again all along the southern coast of Wessex, plundering and pillaging the Saxon shore. In response to this threat, Alfred commanded his new ships to patrol the coastal waters, looking for an opportunity to punish the Viking pirates. Finally, word came to him that six Danish longboats were looting the coastal villages of the Isle of Wight and the shores of Devon. Alfred sent nine of the newly constructed Saxon ships, manned with mixed crews of Frisian and Wessex sailors, to engage the Northmen. The Wessex fleet, after much searching, overtook the Danish longboats as they rested at the mouth of one of the many rivers that emptied into the channel.

The Vikings were caught in a difficult position. The ships of Wessex had effectively cut off their opportunity to sail out the mouth of the river. If they attempted to row upstream, they would eventually be overtaken by the new large Saxon vessels and would only be that much more exhausted for the inevitable combat. And, to make matters much worse, the Saxon fleet had arrived just after half of the Viking force had beached their ships and disembarked to scout out the woods behind the beach.

Thus, as the Wessex ships cut off the escape to the channel and began closing in on the now panicking Vikings, half of the Viking ships sat beached on the shore and unmanned while the other three sat in the water trying to decide how to escape. As the tide ebbed and the waters of the bay slowly drained out, the three Danish vessels still afloat decided to make a run for it, rowing hard for the mouth of the bay, hoping desperately to find some gap in the Saxon blockade through which they could shoot to freedom.

But they could find no gap. All three of the fleeing Danish ships were easily overtaken before they had reached the mouth of the river. Then, in the shallow waters of the bay, the Saxon marines boarded the Viking vessels and turned their Danish hulls into floating fields of slaughter. They cut their way on board, and they waded through the muck and blood-filled bilge of the Viking boats. Significantly outmanned, the Danish sailors were ruthlessly slaughtered, having had little hope of escape. However, since this sea combat unfolded as the flotilla drifted in the ebbing tide, the flood soon drained out of the estuary leaving the longboats stuck fast in the sloppy muck of the muddy river banks. But not all of the ships were equally stranded in the mire. One of the Viking ships was able to break free from the grasp of the Saxon fleet and made for the open water of the channel. By the time they had shaken themselves free from the English sailors, there were only five surviving Vikings left in the ship.

The Saxon ships were all stuck fast in the mud, having been beached by the retreating tide of the estuary along with the five remaining Danish crafts. As the historical account records, they were "very awkwardly aground." Three of the Saxon ships had been stuck fast on the same side of the river as the three Viking ships, which had been previously beached by the Danes who were scouting out the surrounding woods. The remainder of the Saxon fleet was grounded on the other side of the river, leaving the three Wessex ships separated from the rest of their navy. Meanwhile the Vikings who had been exploring the neighboring forest had now returned and, after evaluating the situation, decided their only chance of survival was to launch an attack on the crews of the three Saxon vessels beached on their side of the river.

Seeing the approaching Danes, the Saxons quickly clambered out of their beached craft and made ready for the coming melee. It was a sloppy affair, splashing into combat through the shallow tidal pools and fighting the pagan raiders in the muck and mire of the muddy river bank. Somewhere in the midst of this fight, the tide turned and the flow returned its waters to the bay. By the time the tide began to rush back up the river mouth, filling the estuary and washing clean the bloody gore of the afternoon's combat, the Saxons had forced the Danish pirates to pay a heavy price. One hundred and twenty Vikings lay hewn down in the mud, compared to sixty-two Saxons cut down in the skirmish. As the river climbed back up the shoreline and began to lap at the grounded ships, the crews, seeing that their ships would soon be floating free in the rising waters, turned from the fight to return to their boats. The longboats of the Vikings were the first to be freed by the rising tide, giving them the opportunity to sail free from the bloodied estuary well ahead of the Saxon ships.

The battle on the riverbank had taken its toll on the Viking crews, who were now badly wounded, battle-weary, and numbering significantly fewer than when they had first begun their raiding. As they fled back to Viking-held Northumbria, they were hard-pressed to make progress against the contrary winds and tempestuous seas off the coast of Sussex. Lacking the strength to press on, two of the three fleeing ships were cast onto the shores of Sussex.

Unfortunately for the crews of these two vessels, word had already been sent to the fyrd of Sussex, alerting the shire to the approach of the limping Viking fleet. Thus, as the Vikings stepped ashore on the coast of Sussex looking for a moment's respite, they were greeted by a large armed force, who immediately took them prisoner and marched them straight back to Winchester to be tried by King Alfred in his capital city. Alfred, at this point in his life, was in no mood to extend mercy to these brigands and ordered them hung as an example to any Dane who looked at the villages and monasteries of Wessex with piratical longing. Only one Viking crew returned to Northumbria, heavily wounded and probably ruing their earlier eagerness for a life of plunder.

Strangely, modern historians seem almost universally to interpret this naval encounter as a complete failure on Alfred's part. The debate focuses on the evaluation of the king's new designs for the construction of the Wessex ships, questioning whether the king's innovations were effective. The scholarly bias is inexplicably against the king of Wessex on this issue, arguing that the encounter with the Viking fleet at the river mouth proved Alfred's design was a disaster and a total failure. The point is made that the king's demand for a larger hull, making room for sixty oars rather than for thirty, must have resulted in a significantly deeper draft. This deeper draft, they speculate, must have caused the Saxon vessels to more easily run aground during the naval battle in the shallow estuary, giving the Vikings, whose longboats must have had a shallower draft, the advantage in the fight.

It would be difficult to deny that Alfred's design likely resulted in a deeper draft, though the historical account insists that they were more maneuverable than other ships. But it is impossible to insist that this was the primary reason the Wessex ships ran aground. Even if Alfred's new design did result in a deeper draft, the manpower the new design afforded surely also added significantly to the speed with which the Wessex ships were able to cut off the Vikings at the river mouth, as well as to the numbers with which the Saxons were able to attack the Vikings in the ship-to-ship combat and in the following melee on the beach. Clearly, the entire encounter was a victory for the Saxons, to which the new ship designs contributed greatly, contrary to the miserly estimation of the scholarly world.

Part of the final settlement between Alfred and Æthelstan had been a treaty that formally established the border between the territories of the two kings. Since Ceolwulf, the Mercian puppet king installed by the Danes, had been moved along, Æthelstan now controlled Mercia as well as East Anglia. In the treaty drawn up between Alfred and Æthelstan, however, Mercia was to be divided between the Saxons and the Danes. Although negotiations continued regarding the specifics of this new boundary, the treaty eventually decreed that the border between the English territory and Viking land ran up the Thames, then up the Lea to its beginning. From there the border ran in a straight line to Bedford, at which point it met the Ouse, which it followed to Watling Street. All the land to the northeast of this line was designated as the Danelaw, the territory of the Danish kings. The land to the south and west of this negotiated border was left to

Wessex and Mercia. This remaining portion of Anglo-Saxon Mercia was governed by an ealdorman named Æthelred, who had been chosen by the consensus of the rest of the Mercian ealdormen.

However, by the year 881, the northern Welsh kingdoms of

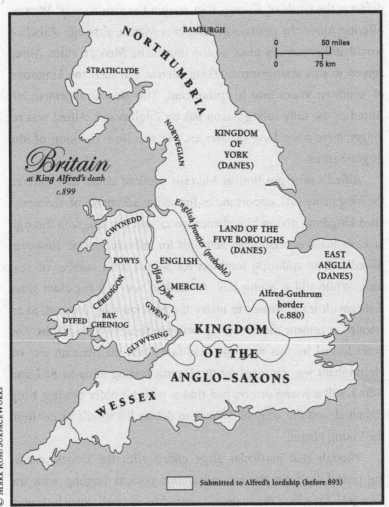

Britain at King Alfred's death c.899

BAMBURGH

NORTHUMBRIA

STRATHCLYDE

NORWEGIAN

KINGDOM OF YORK (DANES)

0 — 50 miles
0 — 75 km

GWYNEDD

English frontier (probable)

POWYS

ENGLISH

LAND OF THE FIVE BOROUGHS (DANES)

EAST ANGLIA (DANES)

CEREDIGON

Offa's Dyke

MERCIA

Alfred-Guthrum border (c.880)

DYFED

BAY-CHEINIOG

GWENT

GLYWYSING

KINGDOM OF THE ANGLO-SAXONS

WESSEX

Submitted to Alfred's lordship (before 893)

© MARK ROSS/SURFACEWORKS

Gwynedd and Powys had allied themselves with the Viking forces who held Northumbria and began to threaten both the southern Welsh kingdoms as well as the remaining portion of Mercia, now ruled by ealdorman Æthelred. After the Mercians suffered a major defeat at the battle of Conwy, they sought the assistance of Wessex, offering Alfred the position of king over Mercia, although Æthelred would still remain in place as the immediate Mercian ruler. Alfred agreed to this arrangement, taking Mercia and then the kingdoms of southern Wales into his protection. This new arrangement left Alfred as the only ruling Saxon left on English soil. Alfred was no longer merely the king of Wessex. He was now the king of the Anglo-Saxons.

Alfred's new position as Mercian overlord could have offered the king many easy opportunities for taking advantage of the weakened kingdom, giving him chances to exploit the kingdom through taxes or make unreasonable demands for military service. However, Alfred had an enduring fondness for Mercia for a number of reasons. While still a young boy, Alfred had watched his older sister Æthelswith leave Wessex to marry the Mercian king Burgred, in an attempt to cement the friendship between these two kingdoms. The bond forged by this marriage held fast when the Mercian city of Nottingham was captured by the Danish raiding army in 867 and Alfred, still a young prince, had ridden with his older brother, King Æthelred, and the army of Wessex to deliver his sister's nation from the Viking plague.

Though that particular siege ended with the Danes marching peacefully from the city with their pockets jingling with the danegeld, for Alfred the siege still seemed to end well, since he found, sometime during that siege, a Mercian bride of his own—Ealswith. Now Alfred offered to renew his commitment to this important ally. He sent his daughter, his firstborn child Æthelflæd, to be the wife of ealdorman Æthelred.

Ealswith had born Æthelflæd to Alfred at approximately the same time the prince had been fighting his first great battle, the battle of Ashdown. This young princess of Wessex grew up in the turbulent and eventful court of her father, throughout the most perilous years of the king's reign. She had been old enough to remember vividly the night the family rushed from Chippenham under cover of darkness during Guthrum's surprise winter attack. And she well remembered the darkest days of Wessex, hiding in Athelney with her parents, ever watchful of the Danish prowlers who hunted her and her family. She had also experienced firsthand the splendor of kingship as her father's ultimate victory over Guthrum and his growing renown had brought fame and fortune to the once-destitute court of Wessex. Æthelflæd was thus a tremendous blessing to be granted to any ealdorman, since with her went the wisdom and experience of the Wessex court, as well as the love and affection of the great king.

Æthelflæd lived as the wife of the ealdorman of Mercia for twenty years, until Æthelred's death around the year 908. Throughout his reign, Æthelflæd proved an invaluable aid to her husband as he sought to rebuild the infrastructure of Mercia, which had been ravaged by the concerted actions of pillaging Vikings and cowardly rulers over the course of decades. Since Mercia essentially formed the bulk of the Anglo-Saxon border with the Danelaw, the rebuilding of this nation was essential to ensure the future safety of the Saxons against the Danes.

Æthelred fell gravely ill with a debilitating illness several years before his death, and Æthelflæd ruled the kingdom in his place. Surprisingly, after her husband's death, the Mercian nation continued to recognize her authority, making her one of the few Anglo-Saxon women to have wielded any sort of political power. Her people lovingly referred to the tough and battle-savvy woman as the *Myrcna hlæfdige*, or the "Lady of Mercia." During her reign, Æthelflæd ordered the remodeling of a number of the Mercian towns into new Wessex-style burhs, following carefully the patterns and strategies she had learned at the feet of her father. This project expanded Alfred's burghal defense system across all of Mercia. One generation later, Æthelflæd's efforts to reorganize and strengthen Mercia against the Viking raiders became the critical foundation for a major Wessex campaign against the Danelaw, which finally dislodged the Vikings from the island of Britain entirely.

On several different occasions, Æthelflæd played the Old Testament Deborah and led the armies of Mercia in battle against the Danes to the north, driving the Viking armies from her northern borders.

Alfred's first son, Edward, was born shortly after Æthelflæd and shared with his sister a clear childhood memory of their terrifying flight from Guthrum's advancing forces. And though the two children shared many of the same dangers in their early years and learned together the same lessons that later shaped Æthelflæd into the great "Lady of the Mercians," Edward, as the oldest son, was still set apart from Æthelflæd, being groomed from birth to take his father's place as king of the Anglo-Saxons. What his sister picked up about kingship and war craft by careful observation from a safe distance, Edward learned in a sometimes dangerously close proximity—standing in Alfred's court, witnessing charters, and personally leading the warriors of Wessex into battle against the Vikings, all before he had turned twenty years old.

In years to come, however, when Edward (later known as "Edward the Elder") was to be crowned king of the Anglo-Saxons, he sent his son Æthelstan to be raised by Æthelflæd. King Æthelstan, having been raised under the tutelage of Alfred's firstborn daughter, would be the king who would ultimately drive the Vikings from his territories, finally uniting all of the Anglo-Saxons under one crown.

Alfred's other children are mentioned less in the historical accounts, so it is difficult to say much about their lives. His second daughter, Æthelgifu, was troubled by an illness of some sort, which forced her to keep her face always mysteriously covered. Eventually, the young princess, troubled by her illness, decided to devote herself to the service of God and took monastic vows as a nun.

Her father had ordered two monasteries to be built—the first was in the marshy wastes of Athelney and was given to a community of monks; the second was constructed at the gates of his Shaftesbury burh, and was given to his daughter Æthelgifu to rule as the abbess. Alfred ensured that the financial support for this institution was well established by endowing the abbey with a number of surrounding estates.

Between the prestige of the royal abbess and the wealth of the abbey's generous endowments, the Shaftesbury abbey's renown spread quickly. Soon Æthelgifu was joined by a number of other women who chose to devote their virginity to God at Shaftesbury. Strangely, Alfred had a much more difficult time establishing the monastery at Athelney since the Anglo-Saxon men seemed far less eager to take monastic vows that would dedicate them to a life of celibacy, prayer, and meditation on the Scriptures. To man the Athelney monastery, Alfred eventually had to resort to recruiting men from abroad, drawing from Wales, Old Saxony, Flanders, and even some of the young Danes.

Alfred's youngest daughter, Ælfthryth, was given as wife to Baldwin II, the Count of Flanders. Even before this marriage into the house of Wessex, Baldwin already had several close connections to Alfred's family. First, his mother was Judith, the daughter of Charles the Bald, who had become the unfortunate young second wife of Alfred's father, shortly before his death. As the widowed queen of Wessex, she had then been shamefully taken as wife by Alfred's older brother Æthelbald in a desperate attempt to demonstrate his own right to the throne. His subsequent reign was brief and tragic. After Æthelbald's death in 860, Judith, now having reigned twice as the queen of Wessex despite being only sixteen years old, sold all her English property and returned home to West Francia. Her dismayed father placed her in the care of a monastery until he could once more arrange a suitable marriage for her. However, Judith outraged her family when the monks who served as her guardians reported that she had eloped with a mysterious count named Baldwin. Initially enraged and set on having the marriage annulled, her father eventually accepted his new son-in-law and entrusted him with the task of ruling the Viking-ravaged coast of Flanders.

Sitting opposite the channel from Alfred's Kent, the region of Flanders had been equally despoiled by the intensifying Viking raids throughout the 860s to the 880s. As Count Baldwin and his son after him sought to defend their shores from the Danish scourge, it was only natural that the Counts of Flanders work in close cooperation with the Wessex king, who was essentially fighting the same battle as the Flemish. As a result of this partnership, the two kingdoms began to exchange defensive strategies and military intelligence. This partnership eventually led to increased trade between the two regions as well as a deeper bond of friendship and cooperation between their clergies.

Finally, this alliance was sealed when Alfred's daughter, Ælfthryth, was given as bride to Count Baldwin II. Of Countess Ælfthryth little is known, except that her husband granted her request that at his death, rather than be buried at Saint Bertin in Saint Omer where only the male line of his family was permitted to be buried, he would instead be buried at the Abbey of Saint Peter in Ghent, where Ælfthryth could eventually be buried next to him. Whatever romance lies behind the story of this shared tomb can only be filled in by imagination.

Alfred's youngest son, Æthelweard, had a very different childhood from his older brother Edward's. Born in the year 880, Æthelweard's boyhood coincided with the peace and prosperity of Alfred's golden age. And while Æthelflæd and Edward had lived their youths as permanent fixtures of Alfred's court, learning how to rule, Æthelweard devoted his life from an early age to learning the liberal arts. If Alfred's will can be taken as evidence of his fatherly affections, then Æthelweard was clearly a well-loved son, receiving dozens of royal estates throughout Wessex at his father's death. At his death, the prince was buried at the New Minster in Winchester, suggesting an enduring favor in the royal court throughout his brother's reign as well.

CHAPTER 7

Alfred the Wise

Alfred found learning dead and he restored it,
education neglected and he revived it, the laws
powerless and he gave them force, the church debased
and he raised it, the land ravaged by a fearful enemy
from which he delivered it. Alfred's name shall live as
long as mankind shall respect the past.

—FROM THE INSCRIPTION ON THE STATUE OF
KING ALFRED IN WANTAGE

A lfred's innovations in his radical restructuring of the military of Wessex, according to the program described in the *Burghal Hideage*, have long been acknowledged as one of the king's most significant and lasting achievements. The transformation of an archaic, clumsy, and unpredictable system of shire fyrds into a swiftly moving, standing army of professional soldiers supported by a network of well-defended burhs, not only resulted in the complete resuscitation of an almost dead nation and a nearly extinct people but also created the sort of national military efficiency that would eventually drive the Danes entirely from English soil. To Alfred, however, the fortification of the burhs of Wessex, the organization of the standing army, and all the great battles won by these newly organized warriors of Wessex were only one portion of a much larger defense policy, which the king had sketched out in his own mind during the frantic years of the 870s.

When the king had searched the tumultuous history of early medieval Britain, he had happened upon descriptions of a golden age, a time when the kings ruled in peace. These were times when the people were moral, with little crime and great respect for their rulers. These were times when not only were their shores free from the raids of pagan plunderers, but the people actually advanced their own territories and extended their borders. And these were times when the Anglo-Saxon tribes were Christian tribes, and not just in name only but faithfully worshiping the God of the Bible with a vibrant and fruitful faith. And the clearest testimony that Alfred saw for their eagerness to worship the Christian God was their dogged perseverance in the discipline of Christian learning.

As Alfred learned from the history recorded by the venerable Bede, there had been a time when the many Anglo-Saxon monasteries were filled with men who were eager to learn to read and write not only in their native tongue but also in Latin, the *lingua franca* of western Europe. These men esteemed the knowledge of God as more precious than any treasure and had therefore abandoned all their worldly pursuits for the chance to study the Scriptures and the heritage of Christian learning. God had blessed these men in their studies such that, during this golden age of British Christianity, the various Anglo-Saxon monasteries and abbeys became veritable storehouses of pious wisdom. Their renown had spread throughout Europe, and the intoxicating aroma of their godly learning had attracted knowledge-hungry men from the farthest reaches of the Christian west.

But things had radically changed during the two centuries that had intervened between the golden age of the Anglo-Saxon church, described by the venerable Bede, and the time of Alfred. The English church had grown complacent, indolent, and lethargic. Numbed by their prosperity, their love of learning grew cold, and their interest in Christian studies died off altogether. Tragically, by the time Alfred came to the throne, he was hard-pressed to think of more than a handful of men who lived south of the Humber river and could read the divine services in their own language. Of the few whom he could name, none lived south of the Thames, meaning Wessex had fallen further into an unchristian ignorance than any other Anglo-Saxon nation. It was virtually impossible to find a churchman in his kingdom who could understand the Latin language.

Now the nation that had been sought out for its treasury of Christian wisdom must travel abroad to seek assistance in understanding the simplest Christian texts. By neglecting the study of the great works of Christendom, the Bible in particular, the Anglo-Saxon people had lost not only the ability to read but more important, the ability to understand the wisdom of God. England, through her intellectual lethargy, was slowly devolving into a pagan nation, a people who neither knew nor served the Christian God.

If this was the case, if the Anglo-Saxons had abandoned the service of the Christian God, then it seemed to Alfred that it was no surprise that God had abandoned them. The king could find in the Scriptures close parallels to the predicament of the kingdom of Wessex. The king of Assyria once conquered the northern king-dom of Israel and emptied the land, leading the Israelite people away captive. The Assyrians then resettled the land by bringing in a large host of settlers, drawn from the surrounding pagan nations. However, when these pagan men and women continued to serve the gods of their homeland, God responded by bringing lions into the land to devour the idolatrous men and women who dared to prac-tice their idolatries on the sacred soil of Israel. It was not until an Israelite priest was brought back to his homeland to teach the pagans how to properly serve the Lord that the lions finally relented and the people could live in peace.

Now Alfred saw his kingdom in a similar light. The nominally Christian Anglo-Saxon people whom Alfred ruled inhabited a land-scape marked throughout by empty and decaying churches; it was a land formerly given over to the worship of the Christian God. The Anglo-Saxons had become an unfaithful people dwelling on formerly sacred Christian soil. Was it any wonder then that God had raised up the Viking scourge, the "lions of Israel," to strike them and remind them of their duties to God? Alfred concluded that the Vikings were not the cause of England's overthrow. They were the result. The Anglo-Saxons' own lethargic apostasy had been the cause of the fall of the various Anglo-Saxon nations. If Alfred was to have a victorious defense policy, clearly armies and burhs were not enough. If Wessex wanted to be successful in her ongoing struggle with the plundering Danes, then the nation must devote itself to a revival of Christian learning and Christian worship.

It had been nearly a full century since the Viking plague had begun with the first tragic raid on the holy island of Lindisfarne. After that disaster, Alcuin had written to the British church urging them to consider this raid as a scourge from God, sent to awaken the Anglo-Saxons from spiritual lethargy. Now, nearly one hundred years later, the king of Wessex finally took this warning to heart and set about reviving Christian learning and worship throughout his land.

As a youth, Alfred had been naturally inclined toward book learning. In particular, the poetry of the Anglo-Saxon tongue, with its haunting cadences and kennings, had cast a spell on his mind that would hold him under its power until his last day. The little volume of poetry his mother had given him had long been a prized possession. The young prince had also had a particular fondness for the book of Psalms and gave special attention to memorizing them, a task made easier by the regular recitation of Psalms in the daily church services. After the death of his mother, however, little attention was paid in the court of Alfred's father to continuing the young boy's studies. Thus Alfred's education largely consisted of a patchwork of memorized poems, psalms, and stock phrases from the church service.

By the time Alfred had inherited the throne of Wessex, he had managed to learn on his own the rudiments of Anglo-Saxon literacy and could, at best, muddle his way through a text in his native tongue, despite having committed countless poems to memory. The

Latin language, which he wanted desperately to understand, had remained beyond his grasp throughout his youth and early reign.

Seeing the deplorable state of his own inadequate education and the general level of ignorance found throughout his kingdom, Alfred set himself to righting this grievous wrong. It was clear that Wessex would need to humble herself and look for help from without. Just as Alfred had looked to the expert sailors of Frisia to train his navy, now the king began searching near and far for the best Christian scholars who could be enticed to Wessex to help that nation rekindle the flame of learning. Beginning in the 880s, the king gathered the few scholars he knew of who lived north of the Thames, Mercian men—Werferth, Plegmund (later to be made archbishop of Canterbury), Æthelstan, and Werwulf.

After enticing these four men to Wessex with promises of countless gifts and places of honor, Alfred secured their services as his personal readers. In exchange for his generous ring-giving, these scholars stayed at the king's side and read to him from whatever books the king could procure. All through the day, and occasionally during the king's sleepless nights, they stood ready to help Alfred make good use of any idle moment in the court, stepping in to read and discuss with the king as many of the great works of Christendom as the king could obtain. These men also worked to buy, borrow, copy or acquire in any way possible whatever books could be found to expand the virtually nonexistent library of Wessex. Since nearly all of these works were composed in Latin, the king's readers had the difficult task of translating each passage for Alfred into Anglo-Saxon, discussing the meaning and implications of the text until the king's curiosity was satisfied and he urged them to continue.

Soon Alfred's community of scholars grew. The king sent messengers across the channel, searching out men of learning on the European continent. The messengers returned with Grimbald, a priest from the monastery in Saint Bertins in Flanders, and with John, another priest from Old Saxony. Though these men significantly broadened Alfred's learning, bringing new texts and opening up new avenues of discussion, the king's mind hungered for more. Next he looked to his west, sending to the monastery of Saint David's in the Welsh kingdom of Dyfed. At Saint David's he found the monk Asser, who agreed, after having been showered with gifts, to return to Alfred's court for six months out of every year, splitting his time between the company of the king and the monastery where he had spent his entire life. The addition of Asser to the king's court was significant as the Welsh monk later became Alfred's biographer and penned the most thorough account of the king's life.

After several years of tutelage under this cadre of scholars, the king began to make significant leaps in his own abilities. Of course his studies, which could only be pursued periodically throughout the busy days when the king was at court, were occasionally completely broken off because of national emergencies, such as the need to lead an army to drive away the Vikings from the front gates of Rochester in 885. Nevertheless, the king continued to progress in his studies. On November 11, Saint Martin's Day, in the year 887, Asser recorded that the king made a significant and miraculous leap, suddenly being able to read and translate the Latin text for himself. Soon the king was fluently working through the church services, reading the Psalms for himself, and working his way through a selection of patristic texts. Now finding himself moving freely

through the enormous body of literature that made up the great
works of Christendom, Alfred's mind instantly turned to the people
of Wessex. How could this great wealth of Christian wisdom be
passed on to his countrymen?

If Christian virtues were to return to England, then the Anglo-
Saxons would need to return to Christian learning. With an eye
toward restoring this learned piety to the people, Alfred orchestrated a tremendous revival of literacy, a revival that culminated in
the greatest literary renaissance ever experienced in Anglo-Saxon
Britain. Alfred later wrote that before the coming of the Vikings, the
churches, though empty of people, had been tremendous storehouses
of books. These libraries had become useless to the Anglo-Saxons
because the books, almost without exception, were all composed in
Latin; and the people of the ninth century had almost entirely lost
their skill in that tongue. The king of Wessex, always drawn to hunting metaphors, likened the many stacks of Latin texts to the tracks
of a wild animal. There were the footprints. If only the English
people could follow them closely, they would be successful in their
hunt, finding that much sought-after ideal—Christian wisdom. But
the people had lost the skill of tracking because of their laziness.
They could make no sense of the jumbled footprints and were useless in the hunt, unable to follow the clear signs imprinted in the
earth, which led to the prize.

Frustrated that such a great heritage had been utterly lost, Alfred
wondered why the Christians of the seventh and eighth centuries

had not translated these works into the Anglo-Saxon vernacular. Had they done so, those books would have not passed beyond the reach of the British church. Then he realized that the Christians of the seventh and eighth centuries never thought it could be possible that the church would ever lose its ability to understand the Latin tongue.

With the Vikings driven from the borders of Wessex and the restructuring of the Anglo-Saxon military well under way, Alfred soon began to find moments of rest from his other kingly duties, moments in which he could turn his attentions to this problem of Anglo-Saxon illiteracy. Soon a plan began to take shape, a plan striking in both its ambition and its simplicity. First, Alfred decided that his goal was nothing less than the literacy of every freeborn man within his borders. If the purpose of recovering education was to recover piety, then it would do no good to educate only a small and exclusive circle of hermitlike scholars, leaving the rest of the Anglo-Saxons ignorant and impious.

Thus, the king of Wessex wanted to see wisdom passed on to as many of his subjects as possible, introducing the radical proposal that Christian learning ought not to be solely the enterprise of the monks and priests of the medieval church. Such a radically ambitious goal was in danger of being so optimistic as to seem unachievable and thus dismissed from the start. The notion that an average Anglo-Saxon man could find the means and the leisure, let alone the necessary motivation, to learn to read Latin texts, was positively risible. So, ignoring the fact that all of the learning of the Christian west had been handed down in the Latin language, Alfred decided to aim for fluency in the vernacular of his people—the Anglo-Saxon tongue.

Schools for the Anglo-Saxon children were established throughout the parishes of the Wessex countryside and were aimed at teaching the very basics of reading and writing in the Anglo-Saxon vernacular in the hope of inspiring a lifelong hunger for learning in the students. The bishops, in particular, were charged with seeking out as many of the freeborn children as could be spared from their other labors to be taught the basics of reading in Anglo-Saxon. Those students who became gripped by the written word and proved particularly gifted in their learning were then invited to press on even further with their studies, turning their attentions from the Anglo-Saxon texts, once mastered, to the basics of the Latin grammar and the immense corpus of works available to those skilled in the ancient tongue. These young men, fluent in both languages, were then better fitted to fill the many vacant positions either in the governing of Wessex or in the Anglo-Saxon church.

Another school was founded in Winchester, a royal school created especially for training the children of the Wessex noblemen. Here, the children of the aristocracy, including Alfred's younger three children (who were still school age) were educated with a rigorous training in the liberal arts, learning their Anglo-Saxon and their Latin, in order to drink freely from the fount of wisdom—the Holy Scriptures and the works of the Western church. Alfred aimed at having the young noblemen of Wessex thoroughly grounded in the liberal arts before they were old enough to begin training in the other necessary "manly skills"—those of hunting, riding, and fighting.

Literacy soon became an essential qualification for office holders in the Wessex government. This requirement seemed sensible enough. How could a man effectively rule the people when he was unable to read the various law codes of Wessex or the dispatches sent to him from the royal court? It is truly a wonder that the kingdom of Wessex had held together as long as it had with so few literate men. For Alfred, the argument for making literacy a prerequisite for a government office went much further than such simple pragmatism.

Alfred was convinced that learning to read would entice the minds of his noblemen to wander through the great works of Western literature and intoxicate them with the wisdom contained therein. Then, having drunk the heady draughts of learned philosophers, theologians, and poets, the noblemen of Wessex would apply their newly acquired wisdom as they worked in their own official capacities and would, subsequently, bring great blessings to Wessex. Like King Solomon of ancient Israel, King Alfred considered wisdom the quintessential kingly virtue. Thus, any man who aspired to a ruling office must begin training himself in this royal skill.

More than any other of Alfred's innovations, this expectation of literacy among the leaders of Wessex met with fierce opposition from his noblemen. Men who had stood in Alfred's court since the beginning of his reign, men who bore on their bodies countless battle scars testifying to their constant loyalty to the throne of Wessex, men hoary-headed and grey-bearded were now told that they must devote their efforts to learning their alphabet and the basics of Anglo-Saxon phonics. Surely the king was asking too much! Despite the fact that the aged minds of many of Alfred's best nobles seemed to resist new learning, the king was resolute in his new demand. Soon the royal court of Wessex was filled with the comic sight of the thegns of Wessex—the same men who had stood undaunted in the shieldwall, standing shoulder to shoulder with the king throughout countless bloody battles—sitting lost in a mental fog as they tried to push their faltering minds through simple Anglo-Saxon texts.

For those who were able to master their letters, Alfred proved to be a generous ring-giver. Their efforts were rewarded with wealth and positions of greater honor. Others, however, could not master this new skill despite the king's prodding and all their best efforts. The king was patient with these men, but firm. If they were able to acquire a reader, either a son or a literate slave who could read to them throughout the day and they were able to demonstrate that they were still capable of tuning their minds to wisdom, though unable to read the texts themselves, then Alfred would allow them to maintain their offices. But for those who proved to have impenetrable skulls, those who could make no headway whatsoever in learning, their offices were forfeited and given to other men more capable of filling the position.

This plan, however, of reviving literacy in the Anglo-Saxon tongue throughout Wessex would be a fruitless venture without a selection of Anglo-Saxon books for the newly trained minds of Wessex to devour. The second part of Alfred's plan to revive learning in his kingdom was aimed at this deficiency. The king and the community of scholars whom he had gathered to his court from abroad dedicated themselves to translating into Anglo-Saxon all the works of Christendom that Alfred considered "most necessary for all men to know." With this in mind, throughout the 890s, whenever Alfred found himself freed for a moment from his "worldly affairs," the king set himself to translating Latin texts into Anglo-Saxon.

The work of translating was always a joint venture, requiring the constant assistance of the courtly scholars whom the king had recruited to Wessex. Each passage was read out in the Latin, then discussed by the cadre of scholars, and finally turned into Anglo-Saxon by the king, in his best attempt to convey the meaning agreed upon by the learned gathering. Before his death, King Alfred personally translated the following into the Wessex vernacular: *Pastoral Care*, by Gregory the Great; *The Consolation of Philosophy*, by Boethius; the *Soliloquies* of Augustine; and the first fifty psalms of the Bible. These works were then copied and distributed as widely as possible throughout the schools and churches of Wessex to provide reading material for the newly literate nation.

Of these chosen texts, the works of Boethius and Augustine were selected because of the constant exhortations given to the reader to turn the mind upward toward wisdom and to value this virtue more than any other earthly treasure. The king hoped that, if this message was taken to heart, these works would awaken a lifelong passion for learning in the hearts and minds of the Anglo-Saxon students. Alfred's translations of these works often varied between what was sometimes a tight correspondence with the Latin text and other times a very loose paraphrase of the complex philosophical works. If the Latin text became overly abstract, addressing knotty philosophical questions likely to confuse the novice reader, Alfred's translations would often break free from the tortuous Latin text, giving his own summary of the general thrust of the text but drawing on the concrete imagery of the Anglo-Saxon world.

Alfred often reshaped the translated passages until they not only used Anglo-Saxon words but also sounded as if they described the Anglo-Saxon world. Human reason became the cable that held a ship floating on a stormy sea to the anchor, firmly fixed on the shore. God, who providentially oversees all of creation, guided history the way an experienced helmsman steers a ship through rough seas. The king's description of heaven sounded just like an Anglo-Saxon mead hall—the king sitting at his table, joined by his many friends who feast with him. But his enemies, sitting in prison, see the fellowship of the king with his thegns in the hall and are, just like *Beowulf*'s Grendel, tormented by the joyous sounds of the king's revelries. The resurrection of the just, the reward that awaited the righteous, was described as "book-land"—a highly sought-after Anglo-Saxon charter that granted a tremendous degree of independence to a land-owner, promising him the right to pass the land on to his descendents in perpetuity. Throughout these works, Alfred sought every opportunity to make his texts come alive for his Anglo-Saxon readers.

Gregory's *Pastoral Care* played a unique role in the king's program of reform. Although this translation provided useful material for any student struggling to master his Anglo-Saxon letters, this translation was truly aimed at reviving and equipping the ministers of the faltering Anglo-Saxon church. Written at the end of the sixth century by Pope Gregory I, *Pastoral Care* was essentially the most widely known and respected manual for Christian clergymen in the Western church. Seeing the terrible state of the Anglo-Saxon church and fully aware of the fact that most of the clergymen in his nation were incapable of reading extensive Latin texts, Alfred created a readable Anglo-Saxon translation of this book and ordered copies produced and sent to every bishopric in his kingdom.

The translation of the Psalms was Alfred's last project, being only one-third complete at the king's death. These psalms, primarily the songs of King David composed throughout the king of Israel's tumultuous reign, had always had a special place in Alfred's heart. Having memorized many of the psalms in his youth, Alfred had used these sacred words throughout his life to embolden himself in battle, encourage himself in despondency, humble himself in his sins, and comfort himself in his forgiveness. The entire spectrum of Alfred's personal trials and triumphs seemed to have been lived out already by the shepherd king of Israel. More than any other text, the book of Psalms had become the poetry of Alfred's life.

Thus, it is no surprise that when searching for the "books most necessary for all men to know," Alfred's thoughts turned to the book of Psalms. This was fit reading material for the king and for the peasant, for the warrior and for the clergyman, for the novice and for the sage. Interestingly, of all the texts Alfred translated, the king's rendering of the Psalms remained the most consistently literal throughout, with very little of the king's own explanatory additions to the text. Alfred felt this was a book that needed little assistance in speaking to the Anglo-Saxon heart.

Perhaps the king's decision to translate the biblical text into the Anglo-Saxon vernacular seemed like an obviously pious choice to Alfred. This attempt to make the biblical text so readily available to the people would, however, put the Anglo-Saxon king in dangerous company long after his death. Nearly four centuries later, the followers of John Wycliffe, known as Lollards, would be burned at the stake for their insistence that the Scriptures should be translated from the Latin into the English vernacular and made available to the laity. Wycliffe's labors at translating the Scriptures into English later earned him the nickname "morning star of the Reformation." When the Protestant Reformation finally reached the shores of England and incited the publishing of English Bibles, the ministers of the newly reformed Anglican church were startled to discover that Wycliffe's translation project had not been the first attempt to turn the Bible into a vernacular. Ecstatic to find so great a precedent as Alfred the Great, the sixteenth-century Anglican ministers began publishing biographies on Alfred and Anglo-Saxon editions of the Bible.

The revival of literacy throughout Anglo-Saxon Wessex brought to life a world of other industries necessary for the dissemination of book learning. The translations King Alfred produced, along with many other translations composed by members of the king's circle of scholars, all required large teams of copyists—the scribes who laboriously generated manuscript after manuscript of these freshly translated texts. Each of these books was produced on vellum, the costly calfskin that served as the paper of the medieval world. The production of vellum soon became its own well-paying industry.

Many of these volumes would be handed on to illuminators, men who decorated each page with dragons, warriors, biblical characters, and the flora and fauna of the Wessex landscapes, painted in painstaking detail with splendorous colors. By the time these books were finally completed, every volume represented a small fortune that had gone into its manufacturing. The industry of book production, which had essentially disappeared from Wessex at the time of Alfred's inauguration, soon was brought back from extinction as a thriving Anglo-Saxon enterprise.

Though each book, having taken weeks of intense labor to produce, already represented a fortune in terms of production costs, the king commissioned the creation of an additional costly gift to accompany many of these manuscripts. The preface to Alfred's translation of Gregory's *Pastoral Care* described this highly valued accessory. The king ordered that his goldsmiths produce what was referred to as an *æstel*, a word derived from the Latin term for a small spear. An *æstel* was essentially a place marker or a small pointer stick to help a weary reader direct his eyes as he worked through a text. Each one of these *æstels* was valued at fifty golden coins (or mancuses) and displayed the height of Anglo-Saxon fine craftsmanship in their delicately wrought gold work. Distributing these place markers to the bishops, Alfred urged those churchmen, who had once lost the ability to follow the tracks of earlier scholars, to pick up these volumes and begin the hunt once more.

Providentially, one of these *æstels* was discovered in the seventeenth century, lying in a muddy wheel-rut only a few miles from Athelney, the site of Alfred's former winter hideout. This *æstel*, now known as the Alfred Jewel and on display in Oxford's Ashmolean Museum, reveals the stunning detail of the craftsmanship produced by the goldsmiths of Alfred's court. This tear-drop–shaped jewel is composed of a recycled piece of Roman quartz crystal, held in a filigreed golden casing, terminating at the bottom in the shape of a wild beast's head. In the creature's mouth is a fitting, which would have held the small pointer rod designed to help the reader closely follow the lines of the text. The back of the jewel, decorated with the design of a tree, is flat, allowing the *æstel* to sit level on the page. Around the edge of the jewel, the gold work forms the words AELFRED MEC HEHT GEWYRCAN, a stunning testimony to the king's love for learning, which could be translated: "Alfred ordered me to be made."

On the surface of the crystal sits the figure of a man grasping two blooming branches, one in each hand. This image was created by Alfred's craftsmen through a process known as cloisonné enamel. In this ancient art, gold wire was carefully bent to form a network of cells or *cloisonné*. These cells were then filled with a glass powder that when melted, filled the gold-edged cloisonné. The significance of the image is still debated by various scholars of the period. The most coherent explanation sees the man depicted on the jewel as an image of Christ, the embodiment of heavenly wisdom, who has come to urge men to turn their minds upward toward the true wisdom from above.

Since the discovery of the Alfred Jewel, a number of other Anglo-Saxon *æstels* have been discovered, all equipped with a socket for mounting a pointer and a flat back for sliding along the page, though none have been as beautiful as the Alfred Jewel and none of the others have been marked with the king's name. Strangely, this peculiar new sort of treasure, a piece of stunning jewelry designed especially to adorn a book, appears to have been unique to Alfred's Anglo-Saxon world. It had no counterpart on the European continent or in later English generations. This was truly an original creation of Alfred's court and a fitting symbol of the king's literary renaissance—a costly ornamentation for the written text.

Alfred's passion for reading and study drove him to other interesting innovations as well. Asser described how the king, after having established a substantial degree of peace throughout Wessex, sought to devote himself more fully to the service of God. As king of Wessex, Alfred realized that it was all very easy in one sense to establish monasteries, to generously endow churches, and to provide books for the ministers. It was all very easy for the king of

Wessex to do these things because he had been blessed with tremendous wealth and power. But Alfred wanted to give a less-trifling gift to God and began thinking about what he could devote to God that would be a more substantive expression of his personal devotion. Alfred resolved that, inasmuch as his circumstances allowed, he would devote his strength and mind to God's service for one-half of each day—spending this time in study and prayer.

The king realized quickly, however, that he could not accurately judge the hours of the day because the sun was often covered by clouds or it set so early during the winter months. Unable to determine the time of day, the king felt that he could not faithfully divide his time as he had vowed, so the king put his innovative mind to work. First, he asked for his chaplains to bring him a supply of wax for making candles. These candles, if made in a uniform size, could provide a timing device, an Anglo-Saxon clock, by which the king could accurately track his hours and faithfully fulfill his pledge.

After a great deal of experimentation, the king finally determined that a twenty-four-hour day could be accurately measured by six candles, each twelve inches in length, made from a portion of candle wax, with a weight equivalent to seventy-two pennies. By burning these six candles, end to end, Alfred could precisely track his progress throughout the day and night. Unfortunately, the king discovered that the gusty English wind, from which the Anglo-Saxon buildings offered only a partial shelter, often interrupted his plans. Sometimes the breeze, gusting through the cracks and thin walls of the king's dwellings, entirely snuffed out his candle-clock contraption. Other times, the steady, blowing gentle winds would fan the small flame and cause the candle to burn inordinately fast, resulting in an unsatisfactory level of inaccuracy in the king's calculations. To combat this, Alfred designed a small lantern made from wood but fitted with sides made of thinly shaved ox-horn, which Alfred had discovered was translucent. This became England's first ox-horn lantern and was used by the king for the rest of his life to help him faithfully fulfill his vow to devote his time to religious services.

It is interesting to note the close parallels between Alfred's work to revive learning in Wessex and his work to reestablish the defenses of his nation. For instance, in both programs the king thought in terms of a nationwide reform, extending to the edge of his borders. His burhs were carefully placed to leave no corner of Wessex more than one day's march from the safety of a fortified burh. Similarly, the king's goal in reviving education was to bring literacy to the children of every freeborn Anglo-Saxon. Second, both programs combined a curious mix of a radically ambitious offense with a conservative defense. The enormous standing army, always at the ready and equipped with mounts and months of provision, constituted an army that in terms of size and nature Britain had not seen since the Roman legions. Yet this tremendously powerful striking force was supported by the system of burhs, a defensive organization that preserved an effective military presence throughout the countryside, no matter how far away the standing army may have wandered. In fact, it was the existence of the network of burhs that made the standing army possible, since no army could be kept in the field when the individual soldiers knew their commitment to a campaign meant their homes were unguarded.

This combination of military offense and defense is nicely

paralleled by Alfred's work to revive learning in the Latin language, along with a major push for literacy in the Anglo-Saxon vernacular. Great rewards could be won by those fluent in the ancient tongue, but learning that language required the concerted efforts of a professional scholar over many years of study. However, literacy in their own vernacular was, with a reasonable bit of work, within the grasp of most of the freeborn men of Wessex. This widespread literacy in the Anglo-Saxon language, together with the translation of central texts into the vernacular, would create a bulwark of learning within Wessex, which would be far more difficult to dislodge from the minds of future generations than literacy in the Latin tongue had ever been.

With the reorganization of his nation's defenses and the training of a literate generation of freemen well underway, Alfred felt a pressing need to begin yet another project that would significantly shape the course of the culture and history of his nation. The king began a major reworking of the various law codes and legal policies of the Anglo-Saxon nations, eventually producing his own *domboc*, the largest and most comprehensive legal code that Wessex had ever possessed. Before the publication of Alfred's domboc, the legal code of Wessex had been a strange and muddled jumble of various rulings and policies of numerous long-dead kings of Wessex, all of which were largely useless to an almost entirely illiterate class of noblemen who were expected to enforce the law code. By the time of Alfred's accession to the throne, legal verdicts tended to be based, purportedly, on an oral tradition of an archaic law code; but in actuality, they had far more to do with the power, wealth, and station of the claimants in the case.

It was just this shortcoming that Alfred's push for literacy among the freemen of Wessex was intended to rectify. Alfred had always assumed that Christian learning and pious living walked together hand in hand. Now that the restoration of Christian learning had begun in his kingdom, it was time to expect pious living to follow. Having taught the noblemen of Wessex, who were entrusted with judging the various legal disputes that arose in the lands committed to their care, to read and seek out wisdom, he could now trust them to study and justly apply a uniform law code. The construction of the various burhs also assisted the king in the creation of this law code. The garrisoned troops evenly spaced in the burhs, spread throughout Wessex, ensured that the strictures of the king's legal code were easily backed up by the might of the king's armies. In a sense, the composition of the domboc really constituted the culmination of Alfred's work to rebuild the defenses of Wessex and to revive learning throughout the nation.

Once more, the king's approach was marked by both conservation and innovation. First, Alfred stressed throughout the preface to his domboc the importance of shunning rash or novel alterations in the legal code. Alfred insisted that justice was an eternal virtue—a virtue defined by the character of God and passed on to mankind through divine revelation. Therefore, hasty and ad hoc decrees that addressed immediate national problems without taking the time to reflect on and consider the eternal principles of justice were fated to end in villainy and abuse. Only those laws that had been founded on the eternal principles of justice, had stood the test of time, had been passed on from generation to generation, and had received the approval of the wisest of counsellors should be enacted and enforced by a just king.

To make this point clear, Alfred began the domboc with a translation of the Ten Commandments given to Moses by God on Mount Sinai as recorded in Exodus 20:2–17. This was then followed by a series of lengthy excerpts of Old Testament case law from Exodus 21 to 23, which illustrated how the principles of the Ten Commandments had been applied in various specific precepts that were relevant to the setting of the ancient Near East.

Next, the king included several excerpts from Jesus' Sermon on the Mount (Matthew 5–7), illustrating how when the Son of God, the "healing Christ," came to this Middle-Earth (the Anglo-Saxon term for the inhabited world of men), he did not do away with or overturn the Old Testament law but merely reapplied the principles of God's law to the problems facing the Roman-occupied Palestine of the first century. Jesus taught the Golden Rule, exhorting men to "do unto others as you would have them do unto you," a principle that succinctly summarized much of the Old Testament law. If a man understood how to apply this one law alone, Alfred reflected, he would need no domboc.

After this lengthy preface, which underlined the king's deep conviction that justice had been passed down from God to men and that it was the duty of law-givers to study Scripture, history, and the counsel of other men as they made their legislative decrees, Alfred finally listed his collection of one hundred twenty laws. (It is suspected that the total number of one hundred twenty laws was chosen to equal the age of Moses at his death, acknowledging once more the biblical foundation for Alfred's law code.) In this domboc, more than half of these decrees were actually collected from the law codes of previous Anglo-Saxon kings, primarily Ine, king of Wessex from AD 688 and AD 726. Alfred and his witan composed only the first forty three of the one hundred twenty laws.

Thus it would seem that the publication of Alfred's domboc signified great continuity with the legal traditions of the king's predecessors. In actuality, this legal code constituted another of the king's great innovations. The novelty of the king's approach toward legal theory is often cited as one of the premiere justifications for the king's unique sobriquet: "the Great." By arguing throughout his preface that justice must be an eternal principle, handed down through both Scripture and the legal codes of the land, Alfred established the framework for what would later be known as "common law," the foundation for the legal system of England for the following millennia, as well as for the legal systems of the former colonies of the British empire—including the United States, Canada, Australia, New Zealand, India, and Pakistan. Alfred was the first Saxon king to give such thought to the enduring nature of law. Ironically, it was just this innovation, this conscious attempt to understand the real source of all law, that drove the king to look for the precepts of his domboc that could reassure the king that his own legislation was consistent with the principles of justice that had been passed on by the healing Christ to the men of Middle-Earth.

When the king of Wessex turned to listing the actual laws of the domboc, he began with the commandment he considered to be "most necessary" for every Anglo-Saxon man to keep, a law that proved to be fundamental to the preservation of English society:

Alfred insisted that every Anglo-Saxon man keep his oaths and pledges. Instead of a prohibition of murder, treason, or some other heinous crime, the king saw oath-breaking as the greatest threat to the endurance of his kingdom. Although this prioritization of the keeping of oaths may seem strange to the modern mind, to the Anglo-Saxon it was clear that keeping one's word stood at the foundation of a civilized society.

To understand the significance of oath-keeping to the king of Wessex, one need only think back on the many times when the integrity and strength of Alfred's shieldwall during the crushing combat depended on the faithfulness of the oaths that his thegns had pledged during those less-dangerous moments of feasting and boasting in the mead hall. Similarly, one can remember the habitual treachery of the pagan Vikings, whose unctuous pledges of peace were disregarded by the Danes within hours of making the pledge. It seemed to Alfred that oath-keeping truly was the virtue that most clearly distinguished a Christian nation from a pagan nation.

The significance of a man being faithful to his word was not just apparent in confrontations with other nations; it was essential for preserving domestic peace as well. In the courts of Alfred's day, guilt or innocence was not determined by the presentation of evidence and witnesses. Instead, the accused needed only to produce a certain number of "oath-helpers," men willing to swear alongside the defendant that he was innocent of the charges brought against him. This may seem naïve, since it would seem easy for a guilty man to find several friends to come and swear an oath to his innocence. By giving so much weight to truthfulness in oath-making, however, Alfred helped to ensure that no man could break his oath without dire consequences. If a man was found to have sworn falsely, he would be ostracized from society, losing his right to weapons, to property, and even to testify to his own innocence in court. Thus, the men of Alfred's day took great care to ensure that they did not make careless oaths or pledges.

After his exhortations toward oath-keeping and his prescriptions of penalties for the oath-breakers, the king turned his legislative attentions to another pressing issue that constantly threatened to disrupt the domestic peace of any ninth-century Anglo-Saxon community: the thorny problem of revenge killings. Again, to the modern ear, this may sound like a rather obscure and arbitrary category of criminal activity to attract such focused attention from the king's new domboc. However, the problem of protracted and bloody feuds had long plagued the Anglo-Saxon kingdoms, a gruesome holdover from their own pagan ancestral customs.

Reaching back centuries into the dark old Germanic origins of the Anglo-Saxon tribes, the English people had long assumed that the only reasonable way to ensure the safety of one's own kith and kin was to wage an endlessly escalating campaign of vengeance for any harm done to one's friends and family. Before the coming of Christianity to the Anglo-Saxon tribes at the end of the sixth century, if a young man's father or brother was killed in a fight, it became desperately urgent that the young warrior seek out the murderer and hack out revenge for his family name, or die trying. Only an unloving and ungrateful son could watch his father slain by another without vowing then and there to dedicate all his energies to seeking out and slaughtering the killer of his kinsman. This obligation extended not only to the fathers, brothers, and sons of the dead, it also passed through the web of lord–thegn relationships.

The bold oaths proclaimed in the raucous mead halls to stand by the lord in the place of slaughter, refusing to leave his side no matter how great the cost, were always accompanied by the additional boast that, if the lord should be struck down in combat, the faithful thegn would commit his sword and his own life to finding vengeance for his fallen lord. Additionally, the obligation to find revenge was mutually binding between the thegn and his master, meaning that the lord was also obligated to seek vengeance for his slaughtered thegns.

Admittedly, in some ways this communal thirst for bloody revenge could be remarkably productive. First, it was certainly a deterrent to some would-be killers when they were struck by the realization that, in giving way to the momentary heat of anger and resorting to murderous violence, a man could arouse the wrath of an entire clan of Saxon warriors, together with the oath-bound lord and thegns. And second, since inclusion in the houses of great noblemen could afford such a tremendous protection by assuring that a man's death would not go unavenged, it forced young Anglo-Saxon warriors to carefully guard their standing within these great houses, making them zealous to be true to their oaths and scrupulous in their faithfulness to their lord's commands. A man cast out of the court of his lord, a man with no family or friends to avenge his blood should he be attacked, became completely vulnerable to the cruel medieval world.

Unsurprisingly, the practice of seeking vengeance for every death, though it may have occasionally dissuaded some warriors from reckless slaughter, still led far too often to an ever-escalating feud, whose final bloody death toll was way out of proportion to the single initial murder that provoked the entire gruesome tragedy. A heated altercation would turn disastrously violent, leaving some poor wretch fatally wounded in the scuffle. His bereaved kinsmen would return later that evening to seek revenge and prove themselves to be true brothers. Of course, the man guilty of the crime would not be easily surrendered by his own faithful friends and family and a second skirmish would erupt, this time leaving dead on both sides. The unquenchable thirst for vengeance would now be rightly claimed by everyone involved, and the violence would continue until the demand for revenge was finally conquered, not by justice or forgiveness but by extermination of entire clans by this insatiable blood thirst.

Seeing the destructive power of the endlessly escalating blood feuds, Alfred realized that something had to be done to curb them. However, in the Anglo-Saxon world, it was understood that the burden was on the victim or the kinsmen of the victim to take the initiative in seeking justice and recompense. The king and his noblemen, though eager to see justice done in the land, normally acted as moderators in these quarrels, not as prosecutors or policemen. Alfred did not want to eliminate entirely the impulse of the Anglo-Saxon men to seek retaliation for the wrongs done to them, since this impulse was the engine that powered the machinery of justice in the early medieval English world. So instead of outlawing the blood feuds entirely, his domboc looked for every opportunity to remove their dangerous potential to escalate into all-out warfare between various clans. Alfred exempted a man who fought to defend his own lord or kinsman in a wrongful attack from incurring a blood feud during the combat. A man who killed another man for committing adultery with his wife was similarly exempt from incurring a blood feud for his bloodshed.

Of course this only touched on a few of the many possible provocations that might launch a feud. To truly mitigate the blood-lust of the retaliating ethic, the king leaned heavily on the practice of replacing vengeful murder with the payment of *wergild*. The wergild or "man money" was a set price given for each man according to his rank, which was paid to the victim's surviving family in recompense for a wrongful death. Thus, if a common freeman was killed in some argument that became violent, his killer could pay two hundred shillings to the surviving family members and avoid entirely the destructive blood feud that would have otherwise inevitably ensued.

Alfred's domboc described in detail exactly how the men seeking the recompense of wergild were to go about extracting it. After a wrongful death had occurred, an Anglo-Saxon "posse" would form and search out the accused. If the man was found in the street and, instead of running for safety, he turned to put up a fight, then the posse was free to strike him down in vengeance for his act of murder. If the fugitive turned and fled and was able to make it to his own house or to a consecrated church, then he was not to be touched. The revenge-seeking mob could stay outside for one week, ensuring that the accused did not sneak away. After the seven days, if the man had not come out to fight, then he must surrender his weapons and go peacefully to the house of his enemies, where he would be held for one month while his family gathered the prescribed wergild to make recompense for his crime. If a family felt they did not have the requisite strength to confront the man who had wronged them, they were free to ask their ealdorman to assist. If he refused, then they were welcome to ask the king to intercede on their behalf and lay siege to their enemy until he paid the wergild.

Of course the wergild legislation, a system of rules and regulations by which a man could seek his revenge, seems almost comical to the modern reader. Sometimes the many strange exceptions to the rules and attempts to anticipate possible difficulties in Alfred's domboc begin to sound more like the collection of bizarre oral traditions surrounding some longstanding playground game at a local elementary school than a serious early medieval legal code.

For instance, if a man was besieged in a consecrated church but the clergy needed the space he was occupying for a service, then the clergy were allowed to find another building in which the man could take refuge. However, Alfred added one important proviso—this new building must not have more doors than the church building. Presumably, this was because the party who was guarding the church building would have allocated their men according to the number of possible exits from the church by which the fugitive might take flight. A sudden shift to a building with more doors could have left the besieging band inadequately staffed to guard the new building effectively. One wonders what previous siege-gone-wrong experience Alfred and his witan had in mind when this law was carefully crafted.

Nevertheless, Alfred's domboc provided an enduring foundation for justice throughout Wessex and, over subsequent generations, throughout all of England. The practice of exchanging the payment of wergild radically curtailed the mounting violence of the blood feuds and, as wrath and vengeance began to give way to mercy and forgiveness, helped Alfred to deliver his people not just from the bloody assaults of foreign raiders but also from their own vengeful blood thirst.

As peace, piety, learning, and the many arts patronized by the king began to flourish under Alfred's rule, Britain began to experience a new type of golden age of Anglo-Saxon culture. Had Alfred only delivered his people from the plundering Danes whom he defeated at Edington in AD 879, then his contribution would have been significant and worthy of remembrance, but he would not have been worthy of the legendary status that the name King Alfred has acquired over the years. He would not have been King Alfred *the Great*.

The king of Wessex distinguished himself from all other English monarchs because, after vanquishing the Vikings at Edington, he set his mind to the task of discovering the true cause of the pagan plague and then gave all his strength to righting these wrongs. The defensive reforms introduced in the *Burghal Hideage*, the revival of learning throughout Wessex, and the new standard of justice required by the domboc, all testify to Alfred's tremendous insight in understanding the true flaws in the Anglo-Saxon culture and the comprehensive solution that these flaws required.

CHAPTER 8

A Final Test

And I go riding against the raid,
And ye know not where I am;
But ye shall know in a day or year,
When one green star of grass grows here;
Chaos has charged you, charger and spear,
Battle-axe and battering-ram.

And though skies alter and empires melt,
This word shall still be true:
If we would have the horse of old,
Scour ye the horse anew.

—FROM G. K. CHESTERTON's *The Ballad of the White Horse*

As Alfred carried out his innovative domestic reforms, he continued to keep an ear tuned to news of the movements of the Danish forces who continued to pillage across the English Channel. The king was certain that at some point in the near future the Viking hordes would again turn their attention to the coasts and river networks of England. The king hoped desperately that his newly constructed defenses would be completed enough to withstand the next onslaught. The attack on Rochester in 885 had proved that Alfred's defensive strategy was essentially sound, but the Danish force that Alfred's mounted army had driven away from the newly fortified walls of Rochester had been a relatively small raiding army. Unlike the larger forces that Guthrum had led into Wessex nearly a decade earlier, intent on wholesale conquest and resettlement of the Christian lands, the small fleet that had attacked Rochester had merely been searching for quick plunder and easily coaxed danegeld. Whether the network of burhs and their garrisoned professional troops would be able to withstand a larger, more concerted effort to overthrow Alfred's government entirely, still remained to be seen.

That test finally came in 892, when an enormous Viking force, numbering many more than ten thousand and dwarfing the previous invading host commanded by Guthrum, crossed the English Channel and grimly resolved to wrest the wealth of Wessex from the Anglo-Saxons and to topple the power of King Alfred and his newly restored government. This new raiding army was composed of two recently united Viking bands. One portion of the Danish army was composed of the remnants of the same army that had led the failed siege attempt against the city of Rochester in 885. After having been driven off by Alfred, this army had, along with a host of other Viking raiding armies, plagued the people of Europe. The following year, in 886, these armies, now constituting a massive force, laid siege to the great city of Paris. So enormous was the host of pagan Northmen who eagerly traveled to Paris to join in the siege, smelling the plunder profit likely to be shared if the city were to fall, that the length of the Seine River was clogged with dragon-prowed Viking longboats as far as the eye could see. The siege, though it lasted more than a year, never broke through the Parisian defenses. The affair ended in 886 when Emperor Charles the Fat bought peace for the Parisians by promising the Viking armies a total of seven hundred pounds of silver, as well as the privilege of continuing on up the Seine, then further into Francia, where Charles allowed them to plunder the province of Burgundy.

The Danes continued to plunder and raid throughout the European continent until the early spring of 892, when a terrible plague devastated the crops and brought the country into a severe famine. Uninterested in starving alongside Europe's peasants, a large portion of the Viking army, a full two hundred fifty Danish longboats, turned their attentions again toward England.

Sailing from Boulogne, the Danish fleet crossed the Channel and rounded the southeastern coast of Kent, turning north up the river Lympne (now known as the river Rother). As the Vikings rowed hard up the river, they encountered a half-completed fortification, which they quickly wiped out, and then settled in at Appledore.

Following shortly after this first fleet, forming what would become a pincer-like attack on Wessex, was a smaller force led by the legendary Viking chieftain Hastein, a man renown for a long and successful career of plundering the unprotected churches up and down the river systems of the Somme, Loire, and Seine. As the various exploits and adventures of the Viking Hastein passed on into legend, however, the most infamous of his bloody escapades was his Mediterranean voyage during the years 859–862. During this tour, Hastein's ravaging took an ecumenical turn as the Viking turned briefly from his typically Christian victims and instead plundered and burned the mosques of Muslim-dominated southern

Spain, as well as those of North Africa. Then, returning to the plaguing of Christendom, the Dane raided many of the more prominent cities of southern Gaul, working his way along the Mediterranean Sea to Italy.

Finally, the Viking chieftain attempted what could have been one of the greatest achievements of Danish brigandage on record, the plundering of the great city of Rome. Seeing that the city walls were much too strong to be stormed, Hastein planned a clever ruse that would take advantage of the Christians' pious gullibility.

First, the pagan chieftain sent a message to the bishop of the city, explaining that the Vikings had seen much hardship and were weary, hungry, and tired. They desired only rest, not plunder. In fact, the messenger explained, the commander of the Viking force had been wounded terribly in their last engagement, such that it was unclear whether he would survive longer than a few more days. And on his deathbed, their chief now hoped that he might receive Christian baptism to ensure the salvation of his soul before giving up the ghost.

The bishop of the great city, having mercy on the pagan raiders who seemed to have come on hard times, granted them the opportunity to buy provisions for their ships within the city walls and welcomed Hastein to the baptismal font, where the bishop stood as the chieftain's sponsor and received him as godson. Later that evening, after the Vikings had returned to their ships, a message was sent to the bishop announcing that the bishop's new godson had died of his wounds and that the Viking warriors, in accordance with their chieftain's dying wish, were bringing the man's body back to be buried in the city. Having received the sad news, the bishop organized a procession of clergymen, noblemen, choristers, and children carrying candles to meet the grieving Vikings at the city gate and then to lead the men who carried the dead chieftain on a bier through the city streets to the church where he had only just received baptism. Once the mournful procession had filled the church, the doors were shut, and the bishop recited the mass. Then the command was given to bring forward the body for burial.

The burial was interrupted when the supposedly dead Viking chieftain leaped up from the bier, snatching up the sword that had been laid beside him, and swiftly cut down the astonished bishop. At this, the rest of the Vikings gave up a blood curdling shout, drew their weapons, and proceeded to slaughter all the Christian members of the burial procession, now frozen in their bewilderment. Then, spilling out of the church and into the streets of the silently sleeping city, the Danes began a gruesome rampage of slaughter and rapine, plundering their way back out of the city and eventually returning to their longboats heavily laden with the spoils of their raid.

The Vikings, who took great pride in their ability to beguile the naïve Christians with their cunning deceptions, had much to congratulate themselves with for this ingenious ruse. At some point during their return journey, however, the Danes discovered a bit of information that dampened their enthusiasm for retelling this tale. As the result of some rather significant navigational errors, it appeared that the Vikings had been slightly mistaken about the identity of the city they had sacked. Instead of plundering the great and holy city of Rome, the pagans had raided the much smaller and fairly insignificant city of Luna, some two hundred miles north of Rome. Needless to say, when this story was retold to later generations, the

beguiling cunning of the Viking plunderers was no longer the cen-
terpiece of the narrative.

Even with the story of the comically blundered raid on Rome,
Hastein enjoyed the reputation of a ruthless savage, bloodthirsty and
plunder-hungry and possessed with a cruel greed for the relatively
unprotected wealth of the Christian church's monastic institutions.
But Hastein had tired of plundering the continent and led his own
fleet of eighty longboats across the channel to England. Entering
the Thames estuary with his smaller fleet, he turned up the Swale,
landed, and ordered that his men begin constructing an earthwork
fortification near the river mouth. By striking Kent on the northern
side, Hastein had carefully positioned his troops near the Danelaw
border, giving him the ability to quickly summon help from the
Danish settlers in Northumbria and East Anglia who were likely to
cooperate with the Viking raid.

Soon word reached Alfred of the Danes' latest invasion. After
hearing the news, the king took some time to consider the nature of
the danger, the possible pitfalls that lay before them, and the wisest solutions to this national emergency. It had been reported that
these two armies did not consist solely of Danish warriors but that
the two fleets of ships had been loaded down with entire Viking
families, along with horses. This could have been good news because
the three hundred thirty boats were not entirely filled with warriors; their numbers were diluted by the accompanying women and
children.

But the presence of entire Viking families also signified that this
army was not merely looking for quick plunder. These were Danes
intent on seizing and settling the Kent countryside. And even after

taking into account the fact that the number of fighting men was less than the number of boats might have first suggested, this was still a much larger force than the army that had conquered Northumbria. Clearly, Alfred must not allow these armies any significant foothold on the British soil.

Thinking that these two powers would be more easily defeated if kept separate from each other, Alfred gathered the might of his mobile army and led his troops to camp directly between the two hostile armies, keeping both of these invading forces well within reach of his own army. However, even worse than making contact with each other, Alfred feared that the freshly arrived Vikings might begin communicating with the Danish settlers in the nearby Danelaw. Since his godson Æthelstan (the converted Guthrum) had died in 890, Alfred had been losing confidence that the Danes living beyond his northern borders would continue to respect the terms of peace between Alfred and Æthelstan. With the presence of such an enormous Viking force lodged deep within the Anglo-Saxon territory, it was likely that many of the settlers of the Danelaw might feel emboldened and return to their previous habits of raiding and plundering.

In an attempt to prevent this possibility, Alfred sent messengers to the Danish rulers of Northumbria and East Anglia and demanded that they swear oaths promising to maintain peace between the Danelaw and Wessex and to resist the temptation to join the new Viking army in raiding the Saxons. The Northumbrians and the East Anglians complied with the king's demands, giving their oaths and, in the case of the East Anglians, six hostages to vouchsafe their sincerity.

However, the oaths of the Danes remained consistently untrustworthy. Time after time, Alfred's army would move to repulse some new foray from one of the Vikings' fortified encampments, only to discover that the Danes' numbers had swelled as a result of the continual flood of eager recruits pouring from the Danelaw to the camps of these Viking pirates. At other times, Alfred's army encountered bands of plundering Danes manned entirely by warriors from the Danelaw, as new raiding armies began to form independently of the mob led by Hastein.

Nevertheless, because of the powerful mounted force deployed directly between the two armies by the king, and the shorter sorties made by the few fortified burhs that stood watch over the lands of Kent, the Viking forces found themselves constantly harassed on every side and unable to carve out a firm footing for themselves in the area. Alfred's ability to keep his army in the field all year round and his well-established network of supplies and reinforcements enabled the king to pursue these invaders with unrelenting ferocity. So far, the king's defensive innovations seemed to be standing up to the test.

Hoping to achieve a swift and bloodless end to the conflict, Alfred sought an opportunity to meet with the Viking chieftain Hastein, who commanded the northern Danish troop. The king was wondering if it might be possible that the same peaceful relationship he had established with his one-time enemy Guthrum could also be established with the notorious brigand Hastein. Eventually, Hastein accepted Alfred's invitations and presented himself before the king to hear the terms of peace that would be offered him. It was a strange

meeting, and for the cynical Hastein, a comic display of the pious
naïvety of the Christian king.

Once more Alfred offered his enemy the chance of converting
from enemy to friend by receiving the Christian faith and becoming the king's spiritual kin. He welcomed his Viking guest to feast
with him, inviting the Dane's wife and children to join them at the
table. Throughout the feasting, the king of Wessex played his part
as the generous ring-giver, showering his wealth and munificence on
Hastein and his family. But constantly the king turned the conversation from earthly wealth to the spiritual wealth of the king's faith,
explaining to the Viking chieftain that these earthly treasures were
but a dim picture of the treasure to come for those who had taken
Jesus Christ as their Lord. If Hastein were to convert to the Christian
faith, he would receive not only Alfred's benevolent friendship in
this life, but more importantly, the eternal friendship of the healing
Savior Jesus Christ in the world to come.

Hastein surprised Alfred with his answer. The Viking explained
that, actually, he was already a baptized Christian. (One wonders
how many times the man had been baptized in various encounters
with Christian rulers who were attempting to reform the plundering pagan.) However, the Danish chieftain was willing to relent and
withdraw his troops from their fortified position. As a demonstra-
tion of his good intentions, Hastein consented to having his two
sons baptized and welcomed into the Christian religion. Alfred, in
return, continued to shower his guests with wealth and arranged
for the baptismal ceremony to be held directly. At this ceremony,
Alfred and his son-in-law, Ealdorman Æthelred, stood as sponsors
for the two Viking boys. In doing so, Alfred bound himself and his

son-in-law to the family of Hastein as the two Saxon rulers became the godfathers of the Viking warrior's sons. Alfred hoped that this spiritual kinship would somehow restrain the Viking's lust for Saxon silver and gold.

At the end of the feasting, Hastein left Alfred with his promise to withdraw his troops, along with a number of hostages to help make his vow sure. Sadly, though not surprisingly, these promises meant no more to Hastein than his legendary baptismal vow to the bishop of Luna.

Although the northern Viking army immediately broke camp and marched north, they stopped short of entirely quitting the Anglo-Saxon territories and made another camp at Benfleet, a village on the north shore of the Thames estuary. From this new location, Hastein launched a fresh series of plundering raids on the surrounding Saxon farms, churches, and villages.

The southern Viking force that had encamped at Appledore, tired of making no progress in their conquest and wearied by Alfred's constant attacks, had decided to move on by Easter. Still wanting to turn a profit on their venture, however, the Viking band chose a bold move. Sending their massive fleet of two hundred fifty ships to sail north to an arranged meeting point within the Danelaw, the Viking warriors set out across land on a ravenous binge of pillage, plunder, and rapine.

Eluding Alfred's army by cloaking their movements in the enormous forest known as the Andred, the Danes drove directly west, straight toward Wessex. Matching their lust for spoils with a frightening speed, the Viking army traveled swiftly from Kent to Sussex and on into Wessex, leaving Alfred and his army far behind and still wondering what had become of the Viking raiders. By the time the Danes reached the borders of Wessex, however, the raiding army had begun to lose speed because of the mountains of Saxon booty they now carried.

By the time the Vikings reached the town of Farnham, just inside the borders of Wessex, the local burhs had mobilized a small force to confront the rampaging Danes. There was little hope that this insignificant fyrd could completely overcome the Danish troops or force any sort of surrender, but there was a good chance that the Saxon band could make enough of a nuisance of themselves to make the hurried Vikings think twice about pausing to plunder the farms and churches of the region.

As the small troop of Saxons was about to charge into the Danish lines, they were startled to discover another, much larger army coming to their aid and joining in the attack. Prince Edward, the elder son of King Alfred, having heard of the Viking army that had escaped his father's grasp, had raised a troop of Wessex soldiers and marched out to check the rapacious Danes. Just as his father had first tasted combat when he, as a young prince, rushed the Saxon troops onto the battlefield to compensate for the tardiness of the king and his army, now Prince Edward, fighting like a wild boar, followed in his father's footsteps and led the charge into the Danish lines, possessed by the same grim resolve that drove his father.

The sudden appearance of the prince lifted the spirits of the Saxons, who fought with an unrelenting ferocity. When the din of the clash finally died down, it became apparent that the place of slaughter had been held by the men of Wessex. The Viking warriors, beaten and bloodied, had fled. The Danish army, with their chief severely wounded in the fray, their provisions exhausted, and their plunder abandoned, had grown wildly desperate and sped for the border of the Danelaw. Nevertheless, it soon became obvious that escape was not possible. Exhausted and beaten, the Danes could not outrun Edward and his pursuing troops, and the condition of their wounded chieftain was worsening: he could no longer endure the traveling.

Seeing the hopelessness of their flight and the impossibility of an easy escape, the Vikings seized the island of Thorney on the river Colne, a short distance west of London, and prepared to hold their ground against the pursuing Saxons. It was a desperate move for such a beleaguered band, lacking the provisions to endure a lengthy siege and too wounded to withstand another all-out battle. Nevertheless, they were about to experience a merciful change in their fortunes. The army commanded by Edward was filled by men who had already served the entirety of their term of service and were now demanding that they be released to return to their homes. Given that the nation was filled with roving bands of Viking marauders, their insistence that they be allowed to return home to protect their families and properties was entirely reasonable.

Additionally, Edward's force, like the Danes now cowering on Thorney Island, had exhausted their store of provisions. Seeing the legitimacy of his men's demand, Edward relented and dismissed the fyrd, allowing them to return to their homes. The prince, however, stayed on with the few men he was able to retain, attempting to keep up a semblance of a siege until the arrival of his father, who was marching west with his army to relieve Edward.

Even with the diminished strength of the besieging Saxon fyrd, the Danes were incapable of making an escape because of the severity of the wounds they had incurred at the Farnham battle. Soon Æthelred, the ealdorman of Mercia and the prince's brother-in-law, arrived with fresh troops from nearby London to replenish Edward's forces. It had become apparent, however, that Alfred, along with the army the king had been leading to relieve Edward and his troops, had been diverted by yet another Viking threat, leaving Edward and Æthelred to negotiate a peaceful settlement with the besieged Danes as best they could.

The Vikings, already deprived of all their spoils and wealth, were eager to purchase a bloodless exit from Wessex by whatever means possible and readily accepted the prince's terms. Edward took hostages from the Danes and received vows from them promising to return immediately to the Danelaw. Though the prince knew even in his youth that these vows meant little to the Viking raiders, he guessed rightly that this band of marauders, though untrustworthy in all things, would be held to their vows by their own weakened condition and eagerness to be free of the pursuing Saxon forces. After leaving Thorney Island, the Danes made straight for the Danelaw, returning to their longboats that stood waiting for them at Mersea island on the coast of East Anglia.

Edward soon learned the cause for his father's failure to relieve him in the siege at Thorney Island. Another Viking army, a host manned entirely by Danes from Northumbria and East Anglia, men who were breaking their oaths to the king, had sailed south, along the eastern coast, with a fleet of one hundred longboats, eager to take advantage of the pandemonium caused throughout Wessex by the Viking raids already under way. This new navy had sailed from East Anglia, down all the way around Kent, past Sussex, and to the far western end of Wessex. Here the fleet split into two fleets, as one section turned up the river Exe and laid siege to the city of Exeter, and the other section sailed around Cornwall, to land on the northern coast of Devon and begin raiding.

Alfred's kingdom was now truly being struck from all sides at once. With these two fresh raiding armies biting into the westernmost reaches of Wessex, another Viking force raiding the northeastern borders from their fortified position at Benfleet, and one more fleet of Viking longboats harbored at Mersea Island just within the Danelaw, where they sat licking their wounds and plotting another attack—truly Alfred's defensive innovations were being put to the test. Had Wessex tried to fend off such an attack twenty years earlier, the Saxon nation would have doubtlessly toppled in an instant, but the kingdom Alfred was building was more than prepared to fend off this seemingly relentless assault.

The raiding army laying siege to Exeter soon discovered, unfortunately for them, that they had chosen one of Alfred's fortified burhs, a city well prepared to resist the Viking attackers. The walls of Exeter, once a Roman fortification, had been thoroughly built up and well garrisoned with troops. The city was well provisioned and more than ready to hold out against the Viking attackers.

Upon hearing the news of the assault on Exeter, Alfred, who had been heading to relieve Edward's troops at Thorney Island, turned

his army to rush to the rescue of the besieged city. Unfortunately, the
king had nearly two hundred miles to cover before coming to Exeter's
defense, leaving the Vikings plenty of time to try to conquer the city,
plunder its wealth, and move on to their next victim. Nevertheless,
by the time Alfred reached Exeter, the Danes had still not penetrated
the city's daunting defenses. When the Vikings, already frustrated in
their lack of progress against the walls of Exeter, saw the approaching king, they gave up hope entirely, hastily returning to their ships
and fleeing.

As Alfred dealt with the attack on Exeter, Prince Edward and
Ealdorman Æthelred heard news of Hastein's treacherous betrayal
as the Viking chieftain began to launch plundering raids from his
new fortress at Benfleet. Seeing that the threat at Thorney Island had
been dealt with, the two Saxon warriors set out to repay the Viking
for his infidelity. First, they stopped in London, where the ealdorman
was able to muster a significant army of fresh soldiers from the city.
Then, this newly formed fyrd marched on the Benfleet fortress.

The Saxons arrived at the Danish stronghold when Hastein was
out on a raid. However, the Viking chieftain had taken only a small
contingency of his plundering Northmen with him on this particular raid, leaving the bulk of the Viking raiding army behind at
Benfleet. The Saxon attack was ruthless and fierce. The warriors of
Wessex crashed through the Danes' defenses in one powerfully punishing charge, overwhelming the startled Vikings and smashing their
resistance in a moment. Soon the Northmen had fled entirely from

the onslaught, and the Saxons were left in possession of the remains of the fortress, together with everything the Danes had abandoned in their frantic retreat. All of the plunder that had been hoarded by the Vikings was recovered by the Saxons, a reward for their combat. The victorious warriors then took their pick of the Viking longboats and sailed their captured plunder back to London and Rochester. The rest of the ships were either smashed up or burned. Edward also ordered the fortress completely destroyed, leaving the Vikings no ready-made defenses for future invasions.

Along with the plunder and longboats, many of the wives and children of the Danish warriors had also been left behind by the fleeing Vikings, including the family of Hastein. What the Danish chieftain had so casually deserted, Edward carefully collected and guarded. As soon as possible, Edward sent these captives to London to await his father's judgment on how they should be dealt with.

When news reached Hastein that the Benfleet fortress had been overthrown and his family taken away captive, the Viking chieftain was undeterred. Moving his camp ten miles east to Shoebury, the Dane continued his campaign of plunder. Soon the Viking camp received a wave of new recruits from the Danelaw, as floods of fresh warriors from East Anglia and Northumbria streamed south to join the Viking chieftain's campaign. It had seemed to the settlers of the Danelaw that Alfred's kingdom must be on the brink of collapse. In the hopes that they had finally found the opportunity to break the resistance of the last Anglo-Saxon king, the kings of the Danelaw continued to send a seemingly unending supply of fresh warriors to join in Hastein's campaign. How much longer could the king continue to repulse such an unceasing invasion?

Thrilled by the sudden supply of fresh recruits and paying little mind to the loss of his family, Hastein pressed on with his plunder. The Vikings, however, were beginning to hold the warriors of Wessex in higher esteem and to search for a less formidable opponent. With this in mind, the Danes marched the length of the Thames, carrying on up the tributaries of the river until the army finally reached the Severn River. The Danes were cutting deep into Mercia, all the way to the Welsh border.

Since Alfred was still in the west hunting the raiding armies that had struck Devon, it remained up to the other British rulers to deal with this new attack. Æthelhelm, the ealdorman of Wiltshire, upon hearing of Hastein's raid, gathered his mounted army and rode in hot pursuit of the Vikings. Meanwhile, the king's son-in-law, Ealdorman Æthelred, joined forces with Æthelnoth, the ealdorman of Somerset who had been Alfred's faithful companion throughout his dark days at Athelny, and the two of them marched their combined armies north as swiftly as possible.

Soon the joint forces of the three ealdormen overtook the Vikings at Buttington, a Welsh village beside the Severn river. Here the Vikings attempted to dig in and wait out the siege. However, the Anglo-Saxon army—helped out by the Welsh who were equally uninterested in a visit from the Danes—were much better prepared than the Vikings to outlast a lengthy siege. The food stores of the Viking army quickly ran out, and the hunger of the Danes began to drive them to desperation. Overwhelmed by the pains of starvation, the Vikings slaughtered and ate the horses the raiding army had brought along, though little sustenance could be gotten from the emaciated beasts.

Eventually, as the numbers of Vikings dead from starvation began to mount, the Danes saw the impossibility of their predicament and hazarded a frantic attempt to break through the Saxon lines, striking out suddenly to the east. But the combined armies of the three ealdormen stood their ground and violently repulsed the Danish drive. The battle was gruesome and cost the lives of a number of Saxon noblemen. Nevertheless, the Vikings were completely defeated. And though a portion of the Danish forces escaped (Hastein among them), the bulk of the Viking army was slaughtered. A mass grave discovered in the nineteenth century revealed the remains of a portion of these fallen warriors—hundreds of skulls and a few skeletons in a series of circular pits, all testifying to the extent of the carnage on that bloody day.

Once again, Alfred's defensive innovations had successfully repulsed the Viking attacks, but this particular siege revealed something new about the real extent of Alfred's success. Not only were the fortified burhs ably withstanding the Danish sieges and not only were the fyrds swiftly and efficiently responding to the summons for warriors, but in this particular siege, the noblemen of Wessex had shown initiative, courage, and a devotion to their people, demonstrating that the king had truly achieved his goals in raising up a generation of principled leaders to govern the Anglo-Saxons.

The three ealdormen, in the king's absence, had identified a threat to the people and had worked swiftly and selflessly to deliver the nation from this danger. It would have been very easy for Ealdorman Æthelred to have excused himself from this particular campaign since he had been continuously and tirelessly fighting for nearly a year and had surely earned a brief respite. But the ealdorman saw that he was still needed and unquestioningly threw himself back into the gory combat for the sake of his nation. An entire generation of English leaders, men who had been trained in the courts of Alfred to understand wisdom, justice, righteousness, and the true duties of a ruler, had been raised up, and the battle of the three ealdorman stood as proof of Alfred's success.

The Vikings, however, were not yet prepared to concede ultimate defeat. Hastein's army, resupplied one more time with fresh recruits from the Danelaw, attempted one last attack on the western reaches of Mercia. Marching day and night, the Vikings crossed to the northern Welsh border well ahead of any Saxon pursuers. By the time the Anglo-Saxon army was able to catch up with the Danish marauders, the Vikings had already found the ruins of an abandoned Roman fortress in Chester and fortified the position against the coming Saxon attack. The Danes had chosen well, as the ancient Roman walls, even in their ruined condition, ringed the Viking raiders with an impermeable shield of defense.

Rather than waste their manpower in a costly assault on the walls of Chester, the ealdormen chose to employ a scorched-earth tactic to besiege the Danes. The Saxons rode down and slaughtered all the Vikings found outside the city walls, removed all of the cattle from the nearby fields, burned up all the corn, and set their beasts to devour all the nearby pastureland—leaving the Danes, once more, stranded and starving. This time the Vikings understood their predicament much more quickly and fled without a fight into the kingdom of Wales, where they were able to plunder much more freely. When, at the end of their rampage through Wales, the Danes returned heavily laden with booty, they carefully traced a high arc across the island of England, staying well inside the Danelaw for the entirety of their journey and cautiously avoiding Alfred's kingdom.

Alfred, meanwhile, was finally successful in dislodging the two raiding armies that had been working up and down the coasts of Devon. The Vikings finally abandoned their hopes of toppling Alfred's kingdom and returned home, sailing back along the southern coast of England, the same way they had come. However, along the way, the Danes decided to make one quick raid on an English coastal town, fill their ship holds with treasure and booty, and give their mission some semblance of success.

The longboats landed on the coast of Sussex, near Chichester, where the Vikings spilled out of the ships and began searching the region for any wealth they could seize easily. Once more, the Danish campaign proved ill-fated. Chichester had been another of Alfred's fortified burhs and was completely prepared to handle this sudden raid. The soldiers garrisoned in the Chichester burh were chomping at the bit to play their part in the great war against the Danish invaders. Once word reached the burh of the beached longboats, the garrison poured out of the fortress battle-hungry. Overtaking the Vikings in the coastal countryside, the Saxons slaughtered hundreds of the startled Danes. The rest were chased all the way back to their longboats, with many more cut down along the way. Needless to say, those who escaped made no more stops along the British coast in their hurry to reach the safety of the Danelaw.

With the western reaches of his kingdom finally freed from danger, the king traveled to London where an important matter waited for him to settle. Upon his arrival in the city, the wife and two sons of Hastein were presented to the king in order for him to determine their fate. The situation was not unlike Alfred's earlier encounter with Guthrum, when the Viking king had been captured after his great treachery. However, what Guthrum had done, he had done as a pagan. And Alfred had forgiven this treachery when he welcomed his enemy to the Christian faith.

Hastein had been different. Hastein had committed his offenses as a Christian man, and his treachery had been a treachery against his own baptism and the baptisms of his family members. Alfred would have been completely justified, in the eyes of the noblemen who sat awaiting his decision, if he had given harsh sentence and sent Hastein's family to their grave or, at least, to slavery. But the king reminded his people that the two young men had become his spiritual kinsmen. He and Ealdormen Æthelred had stood as sponsors at their baptism and had become godfathers to these two Danes. And whether Hastein considered this baptism binding or not was irrelevant to the Saxon king. Alfred considered the baptism binding and would stand by it.

The king embraced Hastein's family as his own. They feasted and once more were showered with gifts by the ring-giver. Then, once they had been loaded down with tokens of Alfred's sincere fondness and reminded of the significance of the oath they had made before God, Alfred provided for their travel, ensuring that they would return safely to Hastein. It is difficult to say exactly how the Viking chieftain took this unexpected kindness. With his family returned, the Dane returned to Europe, never to set foot on England's shores again, leaving the remaining Viking forces to fend for themselves.

For a brief moment in the summer of 894, Alfred's kingdom was entirely freed from Viking invaders, and the king was able to return in peace to his home in Winchester. The Danes continued in their determination to topple Alfred's kingdom and were resolved to make one more try, despite the loss of Hastein's leadership. The remaining Viking fleet, harbored just inside the Danelaw at Mersea Island, set out once more, sailing up the Thames, turning north at the river Lea, and continuing twenty miles north of London. Here the Vikings, in the early winter months, built another fortification and settled in for the winter. One would think at this point that the Vikings' plan was obviously hopeless. All of their efforts to overthrow Alfred's kingdom had failed miserably, and their persistence in what had clearly become an impossible venture seemed flat-out maniacal. It is worth remembering that sixteen years earlier, a Viking raiding army seizing the northern town of Chippenham in the early months of the winter had been able to almost entirely overthrow the last Anglo-Saxon nation. This latest attack employed a strategy that had worked before.

An attempt to drive out the Danes early in the summer by the force garrisoned in the London burh failed to dislodge the Vikings from their fortress and resulted in heavy losses on the side of the Saxons. Seeing the difficulty the men of London were having with this army, Alfred returned to London to carefully consider the situation and help devise a more effective strategy.

First, the king dissuaded the Saxon garrison from attempting another assault on the Vikings' fortress. This would only give the Vikings the upper hand by allowing them to fight from within a fortified position. Next, with autumn approaching, the king brought out a large army that camped near the Danes' position, allowing the Saxon farmers to harvest all of the crops in the region under the protection of the Saxon fyrd. These crops were then taken into the burhs, where they were entirely safe from the plundering of the Vikings, who had been expecting to live through the oncoming winter off of this harvest.

Next, anticipating that the starving Danes would soon be fleeing from their fortification, Alfred looked downriver from the Vikings' position for the right place to build a double-burh. This was a tactic that had been used with great success against the Vikings by the Carolingians. By building a fortress on either side of the river and connecting the two fortresses by a bridge spanning the waters, the Saxons could make the river a death-trap for any Danish longboats traveling down the river. Not only had Alfred avoided fighting the Danes on a battlefield that would have favored the Vikings, he was now starving the Vikings out of their position and forcing them into his own trap.

The Danes had seen up close the effectiveness of the double-burh defenses and knew exactly the predicament into which they had fallen. Exasperated with what had now become three years of failure, the Danes abandoned their longboats and fled. First, the army marched across Mercia and camped at Bridgnorth, on the river Severn, near Wales. As the fyrd followed this raiding army, the men of London seized the abandoned Viking longboats and destroyed the defenses of the Danish camp. The raiding army encamped in a fortified position in Bridgnorth for the rest of the winter, surrounded by the Saxon fyrd, who kept a close eye on the Danish marauders. During this time the Vikings finally came to the realization that their campaign against Alfred had become hopeless. And, just as spring came to the island of Britain, shaking loose the icy grip of a bitter winter, the Danish warriors abandoned their hopes of conquering, or even plundering, the Anglo-Saxon people and resolved to return home.

By the summer of 896, the Vikings had entirely ended their attack on the Anglo-Saxons. Some of the Danes, sick of the life of rapine and slaughter, found opportunities within the Danelaw to purchase land and begin their own settlements, quite literally beating swords to ploughshares. The rest of the Vikings, who still longed for a life of plunder and theft, banded together and returned to northern Europe, hoping to find the Frankish resistance less indomitable than the Anglo-Saxon spirit. However, of the two hundred fifty longboats that had originally landed on the shores of Kent three years before, not to mention the countless reinforcements that had joined the Viking campaign throughout those years, the Danes who returned to France in 896 could scarcely fill five longboats. Truly, the spirit of the Vikings had been broken by the kingdom Alfred had built.

Three years later, in the year AD 899, six days before All Hallows' Day, King Alfred died. Having reigned twenty-eight and a half years, he died at the age of fifty. What may sound like a short life to the modern reader would actually have been considered a long and full life to Alfred's contemporaries. Asser, Alfred's friend and biographer, related how, especially in these later years, Alfred was often severely tortured by the pains of some unknown illness. Thus it is likely that Alfred's death was neither unexpected nor untimely. The king was buried in the Old Minster of Winchester, though his bones would be repeatedly moved during the following centuries.

After Alfred's death, the holdings of the king of Wessex were steadily expanded by Alfred's son, Edward, and his grandson, Æthelstan, until soon the throne of Alfred came to rule over the entirety of the island of Britain. Even though Æthelstan is often referred to as the first king of England because all of England was first united under his reign, the accomplishments of Æthelstan and Edward were really just the natural culmination of the reforms first established during Alfred's reign. Alfred truly was the great king of England, the one monarch who rightly understood the needs of the nation and unrelentingly gave all he had to supply those needs.

England, and the many nations descended from her, still have Alfred to thank for a substantial portion of the heritage and freedoms that they enjoy today. The title "Alfred the Great," so strangely offensive to the modern ear, was well deserved by the Anglo-Saxon warrior-king. Of course these words of unreserved praise are all in need of much qualification. Alfred was, after all, a mere mortal and certainly had his fair share of foibles. Nevertheless, he was a fierce warrior, a devout Christian ever thirsting for wisdom, deeply committed to justice, a lover of mercy, and a king who gave himself for his people. He was practically a myth and a much-needed reality. He was the king of the Whitehorse—Alfred the Great.

© GORILLA POET PRODUCTIONS

Acknowledgments

This book is the fruit of my studies for an MA in English literature at the University of Idaho, under Dr. Rick Fehrenbacher. Although utterly unlike my dissertation for that degree, a translation and commentary on Alfred's version of Augustine's *Soliloquies*, most of my appreciation for Alfred flows from my research for that project, as well as from Dr. Fehrenbacher's infectious love for Anglo-Saxon literature. Many thanks to Aaron Rench for getting me into this. And many more thanks to my wife and children, who have richly blessed me throughout this work.

All translations, and any silly mistakes, are my own.

About the Author

Benjamin R. Merkle is a Fellow of Theology and Classical Languages at New Saint Andrews College and a contributing editor to Credenda/Agenda. He received an MA in English literature from the University of Idaho and an MSt in Jewish Studies at the University of Oxford, and is currently pursuing his doctorate at the University of Oxford.

Annotated Bibliography

GENERAL ANGLO-SAXON HISTORY

The Anglo-Saxons, James Campbell, Penguin: New York, 1991.

A very good place to start with any studies in the Anglo-Saxon era
   is the helpful, and beautifully depicted, introduction written by
   James Campbell.

Anglo-Saxon Chronicle, trans. Michael Swanton, Routledge: New
   York, 1998.

The premier primary source for this era is the Anglo-Saxon
   Chronicle, a year by year accounting of the events considered
   most significant to the recorders of early English history.

GENERAL BIOGRAPHY OF ALFRED

Alfred the Great: War, Kingship and Culture in Anglo-Saxon England,
   Richard Abels, Longman: Harlow, 1998.

The best scholarly biography available is by Richard Abels,
   Professor of History at the U.S. Naval Academy.

King Alfred the Great, Alfred Smyth, New York: Oxford Press, 1995.

Another very informative biography is offered by Oxford Press,
   authored by Alfred Smyth.

However, Smyth is convinced that the primary source for our
   knowledge of the life of Alfred, namely the biography produced
   by Asser, is a late forgery. Convinced that most of what we

know about Alfred is a hagiographical manipulation of the facts, Smyth dedicates himself to exposing the real Alfred to his readers. Nevertheless, Smyth's work is still a treasure trove for the historical background to Alfred's reign. His previous publications on the Vikings of this era (works like *Scandinavian Kings in the British Isles 850-880* and *Scandinavian York and Dublin: The History and Archaeology of Two Related Viking Kingdoms*) are also invaluable for understanding the context of Alfred's reign.

Alfred the Good Soldier, John Peddie, Bath: Millstream Books, 1992. John Peddie's biography focuses primarily on Alfred's campaigns, and carefully retraces likely routes of travel and the chronologies of Alfred's many battles.

ALFRED'S LITERARY WORKS

Alfred the Great: Asser's Life of King Alfred and Other Contemporary Sources, Simon Keynes and Michael Lapidge, trans., Penguin: New York, 1983.
Simon Keynes and Michael Lapidge have translated a selection of excerpts from Alfred's works, along with the full text of Asser's biography of the King and a number of other contemporary sources.

Bately, Janet. "The Books That Are Most Necessary for All Men to Know: The Classics and Late Ninth-Century England, A Reappraisal" in *The Classics in the Middle Ages: Papers of the Twentieth Annual Conference of the Center for Medieval and Early Renaissance Studies*, eds. Aldo Bernardo and Saul Levin. Binghamton: Center for Medieval and Early Renaissance Studies, 1990.

————. "The Alfredian Canon Revisited," in *Alfred the Great: Papers from the Eleventh Centenary Conference*, ed. Timothy Reuter. Ashgate: Burlington, 2003.

————. "The Literary Prose of King Alfred's Reign: Translation or Transformation?" *Old English Newsletter Subsidia* vol.10, 1984.

Whitelock, Dorothy. "The Prose of Alfred's Reign," *Continuations and Beginnings*, Thomas Nelson and Sons: London, 1966.

For understanding the import of Alfred's writings, the work of Dorothy Whitelock and Janet Bately are invaluable.

Reforms of the Infrastructure

Fortifications in Wessex c. 800-1066, Ryan Lavelle, Osprey: Oxford, 2003.

Alfred's Kingdom: Wessex and the South, 800-1500, David Hinton, Dent and sons: London, 1977.

Alfred's contribution to the infrastructure of England is nicely illustrated in these two volumes.

Museums

Sutton Hoo exhibit at the British Museum in London

Anglo-Saxon treasures of the Ashmolean Museum of Oxford (especially the Alfred Jewel)

Winchester museum in Alfred's capital city

No real study of Alfred the Great or Anglo-Saxon England is complete without a firsthand encounter with the beautiful artefacts of early medieval England. I highly recommend these museums.

Index